T0086234

Full
Glass **Living**

28 Days to Dump
Limiting Beliefs

AKITA BROOKS

BALBOA.PRESS
A DIVISION OF HAY HOUSE

Scripture quotations marked "NCV" are taken from the New Century Version, Copyright © 1987, 1988, 1991 by Word Publishing, a division of Thomas Nelson, Inc. Used by permission. All rights reserved.

Scripture quotations marked NKJV are taken from the New King James Version. Copyright © 1982 by Thomas Nelson, Inc. Used by permission. All rights reserved.

Balboa Press books may be ordered through booksellers or by contacting:

Balboa Press
A Division of Hay House
1663 Liberty Drive
Bloomington, IN 47403
www.balboapress.com
1 (877) 407-4847

Because of the dynamic nature of the Internet, any web addresses or links contained in this book may have changed since publication and may no longer be valid. The views expressed in this work are solely those of the author and do not necessarily reflect the views of the publisher, and the publisher hereby disclaims any responsibility for them.

The author of this book does not dispense medical advice or prescribe the use of any technique as a form of treatment for physical, emotional, or medical problems without the advice of a physician, either directly or indirectly. The intent of the author is only to offer information of a general nature to help you in your quest for emotional and spiritual well-being. In the event you use any of the information in this book for yourself, which is your constitutional right, the author and the publisher assume no responsibility for your actions.

Any people depicted in stock imagery provided by Getty Images are models, and such images are being used for illustrative purposes only. Certain stock imagery © Getty Images.

Print information available on the last page.

ISBN: 978-1-9822-4977-9 (sc)
ISBN: 978-1-9822-4979-3 (hc)
ISBN: 978-1-9822-4978-6 (e)

Library of Congress Control Number: 2020911051

Balboa Press rev. date: 07/30/2020

CONTENTS

PART I

PART II
Spirituality

PART III
Self Esteem

PART IV
Health

PART V
Free Time

PART VI
Relationships

PART VII
Finances

PART VIII
Creative Expression & Success

DEDICATION

For the INSPIRATION to write this book given to me
by God, Divine Love, the Christ-Consciousness, He who
cannot be defined by human words or expression.

For the MOTIVATION to write this book for my
son, D.J. I'm leaving you a legacy of my own life
experiences, that you may be stronger for it.

EPIGRAPH

"First make the inside of the cup clean, and then the outside of the cup can be truly clean." Matthew 23:26 NCV

FOREWORD

I met Akita Brooks for the first time when she came to our church. She was by all accounts, from my point of view, a bright and shining light of positivity. After some time, Akita disappeared from our congregation only to reappear about 2 years later. In getting to know Akita anew, following her Full Glass Living Program on Facebook and reading this book, I now have a deeper understanding of her journey and those missing years. She is currently very active in her "Full Glass Living" approach to life as she follows the inspirations she receives from God. I am incredibly grateful to say that some of those inspirations have led her to become an active and integral part of our church family and I am so grateful!

The life experiences so vulnerably shared by Akita are a testament to the empathy of her loving heart which is the inspiration for this book. Her desire to draw upon her own life experiences to help others is to be commended.

Full Glass Living is an easy to read very relatable guide to just that - full glass living! Living a full, happy, and productive life. Knowing that every event, situation, and circumstance we find ourselves in is an opportunity to learn and grow. Akita does a beautiful job of relaying this along with some tips and guidelines of how to achieve it.

I love the concept that I am the glass. What kind of glass am I determines my capacity to hold water; water being the stuff life is made of. I call it the substance of God which is all around me and out of which I create my life. What I create is based upon my perception of the glass and the things I am holding in it. I can change the glass at any time. I can dump what is in the glass and get busy re-creating if I am not happy with what is in it.

But do I always need to be busy, filling the glass to the brim with creating and re-creating, or do I perhaps need to leave space to create in? Space to allow myself time to rest, observe and soak it all in so I can be renewed and inspired to get busy again. When we get so busy that we lose the focus of 'purpose' in the 'doing' our minds become cluttered and we become lost in the process. Things become unclear, clouded by everyday living and the responsibility it bears, much of which we thrust upon ourselves making life more difficult.

Then there is the Pitcher from which we refill our glass. Ah, yes! The unlimited, ever full Pitcher of Truth. What is our perception of the Pitcher? How do we open ourselves to the realization that the Pitcher is never empty? How do we empty the stagnant water in our glass to make room for the crisp, clear, unlimited Living Water of the Pitcher?

Akita has put together a 28-day program in which we question our current beliefs, then use denials, affirmations, and specific actions to help us 'dump' the old for the refreshing, revitalizing new. In her words it's a planning system designed to manage the pieces of your life and align them with what you truly want. But first you must get clear on what it is you want. What is my heart's desire and how do I get there?

The Full Glass Living program is concise and easy to follow. It can help the reader begin to build a daily practice of recognizing and "dumping" old thinking and behaviors, taking time to see what is in the "space" of their glass, and then to refill and renew their spirit from the pitcher of Divine Love and Life.

I highly encourage you to put this program into practice and see what it can do for your life! Open your mind and heart to the truth that the glass is not half empty or half full...the glass is FULL! And you are the glass! A perfect container for the substance of life and love to manifest in and through from the unlimited Fount of the Pitcher.

Reverend Rebecca Galati

PREFACE

F ull *Glass Living: 28 Days to Dump Limiting Beliefs* is about
releasing the limiting beliefs that hold us back because we're
too afraid of messing up, worrying about what others will
think of us, and worried about what we think of ourselves. We
can be riddled with stress, worry, and defeat before we even begin
the process of moving towards our own good. This book is a
raw exploration and sharing of these concepts. Though I share
quite often from my practical Christian faith, this book was not
originally intended to be a spiritual book, per se. I believe God
had other plans. As I continued to write, the evolution of the book
shifted from *my* original plans. He is truly working through me,
to use my life experiences and hardships as an example of being a
child of God while also realizing that troubling things do happen
to us. We need to overcome these experiences and not grip a
hold of our life to the point that we're not moving forward to
the good we deserve. This is not possible without looking at the
full spectrum of one's life. The limiting beliefs about our mental,
emotional, physical, and, indeed, spiritual aspects of abundance
are waiting to be released. Perhaps, for those who are emotionally
sensitive and/or struggle with mood disorders, this may be more
of a challenge. I tried to deny and fight against these struggles
instead of surrendering to what is, so that I could move through

them. In fact, I was afraid to even approach this book with such vulnerability about my journey, that I procrastinated for three years to complete it. However, how can I teach, coach, and write a book about releasing limiting beliefs if I remain stuck in my own? Hence the release. I'm ready to share, so here we go...

ACKNOWLEDGEMENTS

I could not have completed Full Glass Living without the help of my tribe who have encouraged and inspired me along the way. First to Douglas Bland Jr, my son who gives me the motivation to be the best mother possible. You've taught me patience, understanding, and the miracle of life. You've also encouraged me to share the lessons that I wished I understood with clarity a long, long time ago. I'm in awe of God's blessing to me.

My parents, Charles and Linda Brooks who enfold me with the human expression of unconditional love. You both are my rock during turbulent times of struggle, and have always entertained my creative, expressive spirit. My acknowledgement and dedication would be incomplete without professing the unfailing love that my grandmothers Mary McLemore and Ruth Brooks bestow upon me. The qualities of strength, resilience, and love I only hope to embody as an example to others, as you both have been for me.

I want to acknowledge the many friends and mentors who supported me through this journey of capturing the essence of what I wanted to share and say. My best friend Mary Walsh, who offers just a little nudge whenever I question or hold back in using my voice. You have also provided invaluable insight to the final developmental edits of this book. Leo Campbell, who keeps me honest and never hesitates to put a mirror in front of me as a reminder of God's greatness working through me. You both are my spiritual sister and brother and I love you dearly.

Reverend Rebecca Galati, Margaret Atkins, and Kate Klisch who also provided much feedback and support in the development of this book, and to the rest of the Unity Church of Christ family for always offering me loving arms and support in my journey of faith. My cherished family, friends and masterminds who offered sage advice, cheered me on, and fanned the flames under me to complete this book in ways you may not have realized. For these things, I am eternally grateful to you all.

I also thank editors Cynthia and Ilana for cleaning up my literary blunders and offering feedback to further develop my writing. Finally, I can't forget to thank Balboa Press for the consistent follow-up over the years in the development and final completion of my manuscript. Your team has kept me honest about my true goals and helped me stay on course.

INTRODUCTION

How to Use This Book

To get the most out of your reading, I suggest you take your time. Let the concepts melt into your mind for a while before moving to the subsequent chapters or sections. You may also want to read the book while watching the free *Full Glass Living Companion Course* found at **fullglassliving.com**. Or, you may want to review the concepts and watch the course after reading the entire book the first time. In Part I, we will set foundations for Full Glass Living, by examining several perspectives as well as the metaphors of The Glass, The Water, and The Pitcher. Finally, in Parts II-VIII, we will look at common limiting beliefs in various aspects of our life, then dump them for beliefs that support our wellbeing. We'll practice day-to-day activities to craft a life built on the Full Glass Perspective and the continual clearing of error thinking.

I suggest that you read the entire book first, then jump around and review the most pressing topics of concern in your life. Remain fluid and open to the ideas and concepts presented here. If you do, you will find a new way of looking at your life and can curate one that will move you forward towards your goals. I am so honored to be your guide in this process and enthusiastic about what you are about to read! I welcome you to share your insights, comments, and the changes you see in your life with me.

So, let me be clear. Even as a certified stress management coach and an academic mastering various aspects of complementary therapies that support our life, I may not have all the answers to life's biggest questions. What I can say is that in my life, I struggled with limiting beliefs about my being since I was a little girl. With fear and doubt. And now, as an adult approaching my late forties, I find a little less of a struggle. I'm more enlightened than that little girl. My intent for this book is to offer a guide for those who are especially emotionally sensitive or anyone who has ever felt the grip of limiting beliefs and emotions get in the way of the successes they truly would like to see in their life. This guide is as important for me as it is for the person reading it. I'm honored that you're going to read the pages I'll share with you. I'm going to help you explore. Also, I'm going to share tools that have helped me in times of trouble and that have supported a balance in my wellness. I can't say that I always have it all together—I certainly don't. What I can say is that I'm a human being living in this human existence, and there is a better way.

The inspiration for Full Glass Living came to me a few months after having major surgery. Just two days after the Christmas holiday of 2013, I felt like I was having a heart attack. My mother helped me seek medical attention. What we eventually found out was I had an enlarged thymus gland. My surgeon explained that though this is a rare case, there were two options for surgery; one option would be a robotic surgical procedure, by a small incision in my chest, to pull the darn thing out, and the other option was equivalent to open-heart surgery, a sternotomy. They would have to cut my sternum and open me up. After a call from my surgeon a few days later, he confirmed that I was not a candidate for the less invasive option. On March 18, 2014, I had a thymectomy via sternotomy.

When I first got diagnosed with the hyperplasia of my thymus gland, I petitioned to God. *What have I done? Please take this away. Why is this happening to me?* You see, for a couple of years before, I felt like something was wrong. I was divorced. I was working on raising my son, but physically, I didn't feel right. I tried all sorts of things to get my physical health together, from exercising to eating right, but it was always a struggle. I was also feeling strange sensations within my body and in my mind. At the time, I was involved in a relationship that seemed so beautiful, but one I didn't need to be in. My emotional and spiritual health was wrecked. However, as I lay getting ready for surgery, and by the time I had to take that surgery, I felt great. My house was in order. I was ready to die. I was ready to meet God. I was okay.

So, here I am writing a self-help book. Maybe it should be called a self-coaching book because the idea for Full Glass Living is about how you can use tools to empower yourself and work on your limiting thoughts that askew the view of your life. Having a coach walk you through this would be an amazing thing. There is nothing like having someone to help you unpack the stuff that you're trying to sort out for your life's goals. This book would be the next best thing.

Again, this is an ongoing journey for me. I've realized that as an enlightened Warrior, as someone who is emotionally sensitive, empathetic, and intuitive, I do an excellent job of supporting other people. If you need something done, I'm your girl. I'm really good at taking care of others and making sure that they get what they need. But I absolutely suck at taking care of myself. Or at least I did. And I'm more aware now when I need self-care. I think because of the way I am, because I feel so deeply, I feel others' pain, and I was hyper-sensitive to the intolerances in the world and the injustices. I often had to take breaks and shield myself from the negative energy that swirls around in society. Therefore, I don't feel guilty when I need extra time for self-care or when to take a break from work. I have the intensity of taking care of others, but equally so, I need to take care of myself with that same amount of intensity.

Is the Glass Half-Full or Half-Empty?

I take an expanded look at this proverbial question and challenge the traditional approach that the answer must be one or the other. I encourage you to dismiss the idea that there is half of anything! If you think of the glass as half-empty, this is the *pessimistic perspective* that there isn't enough "stuff," that maybe *this* is all there is at the moment. This is a disempowering way to look at life and perhaps creates a vicious cycle of doubt, worry, disappointment, and fear. Not a fun time for us emotionally sensitive types too! Conversely, if you look at the glass as half-full, you take an *optimistic perspective* that you've got something good going and that perhaps there is more out there than what you have at present. Not a bad way to look at life, and it can certainly lead towards reaching life goals.

What I present in this book is something different. How about looking at the glass as *always* full? Usually, when we look at the glass, we see only the water. We totally forget that the remaining part of the glass, indeed the leftover space, is filled with air made up of various gases and...(drumroll, please)...water vapor! In Full Glass Living, we adopt the *enlightened perspective* that both the water and space are vitally important to sustain life! Plus, there is so much more going on with the big picture, such as caring for your glass and how you get more water when you need it. Fear does not have to hold a grip on us when we realize that the glass is always full.

I initially wrote this book for those sensitive individuals in the hospitality and service industries who may constantly feel like their own glass is at the half-mark. Coming from the hospitality industry, I know we can give so much of ourselves, physically and emotionally, to always be on show, but feel like we lack the time and energy to take care of ourselves. This doesn't make a lot of sense. How can people dedicated to the service of others fail so miserably in creating a wholesome life of their own? As a person who suffered from stress, burnout, and depression, I'm especially passionate about the concepts provided in this book. I've also seen many of my colleagues, students, and clients struggle with the issues of navigating their emotions and creating the life they want. As they juggle the many facets of their commitments, I've found they've lacked the positive means to cope. My charge in sharing the concepts of this book is to create the space for us to have the life we want, while still giving of ourselves to others. What you will find are principles I apply in my own life, and I wholeheartedly encourage you to test them on your own.

Using my emotionally sensitive baggage in this writing is meant to be a teaching memoir, that you may discover aspects of your story by means of hearing my story. To do just that, let's start with Chapter 1.

PART I

CHAPTER 1

What is Full Glass Living?

Trying to Cope When the Glass is Empty (Trigger Warning)

As mentioned before, sometimes our emotions get in the way of the healthy perspective we can see about life. I know that for me, this has happened in some serious times in my life. It was difficult to see all the goodness that was right in front of me! It was like I was wearing distorted glasses. My mood and emotions allowed me to only see the glass as empty. In this state, feelings of guilt, fear, powerlessness, worry, and loss usually prevail. I needed to get extra help. It was like one side of my mind was telling me that this was not logical, yet my heart was feeling empty. I could be the observer, watching myself be miserable and reveling in it!

It can be hard to get out of this state on one's own. I was able to do it with self-awareness, knowing when I needed extra support, and asking. Asking was so hard for me. I didn't want to impose on anyone. I didn't want anyone to know my dirty secret, at least this one. That I was a "phony." Living life as if all is good with a smile on my face, when inside I couldn't shake the dread of unhappiness. God help me! I felt my life was spinning out of control, into chaos. In her book, *Leadership and the New Science: Discovering Order in a Chaotic World*, Margaret J. Wheatley (2006) says that, "in the midst of chaos, there is still an order of predictability, that both live with each other." Could my experiences be well-ordered and chaotic at the same time? Wheatley further shares:

> "Most of us have experienced this ride of chaos in our own lives. At the personal level, chaos has gone by many names, including 'dark night of the soul' or 'depression.' Always, the experience is a profound loss of meaning, nothing makes sense in the way it did before; nothing seems to hold the same value it once did. These dark nights have been well-documented in many spiritual traditions and cultures. They are part of the human experience, how we participate in the spiral dance of form, formlessness, and new norm. As we reflect on the times when we personally have descended into chaos, we can notice that as it ends, we emerge changed, stronger in some ways, new. We have held in us the dance of creation and learned that growth always requires passage through the fearful realms of disintegration."

Distorted Vision

The sense of fear, especially in the depths of deep depression, is quite familiar to me—all too familiar. The first time that I was acutely depressed was when I was married. I felt like something was wrong. I felt empty, and I knew that the marriage wasn't working. In fact, I knew six months after being married that something was off. By four years into the marriage, it all started to come to a head. I was feeling deeply sad and unfulfilled in my home life. The only thing I felt good about was having my son and being able to take care of him. Even that was a struggle. I felt like I wasn't good enough as a mother to take care of him. I remember sitting in the kitchen one day, and my husband, at the time, stood my son in front of me and said, "Listen, you need to live, for him." I remember saying to him, "There's other people, another woman who could take care of him and do better than I can." I started giving up.

When I started seeing a therapist and started having conversations, it was only after a couple of sessions when I realized that part of the root of my unhappiness was with my marriage. I also was taking a self-help program for anxiety and depression, in addition to medication. Please know that I don't have anything against medication. The medication at the time gave me enough support to be able to clear the dark clouds that seemed to follow me. It gave me enough clearance to see and think about what was going on in my life. Even though the medication made me incredibly tired, it was very hard to get up to go to work and get through my day, but it did help. I remember being so depressed, having thoughts of waiting for a train and taking a step onto the tracks, to be done with it, hoping that in an instant, my pain would end.

This wasn't the first time I had such thoughts. When I was a child, I remember standing in the kitchen of my family home, contemplating my demise by my own hand. I paused, waiting, wondering if this was something I *really* wanted to do. I had the sense that maybe my parents or brother and sister would walk in and ask what I was doing. Looking back, it was my first glimpse at a poor choice as a cry for help. Perhaps for anyone who's ever attempted suicide, that's all they really wanted. To be heard and for someone to take care of them. For the pain to stop.

Of course, there are other reasons why people will commit acts of desperation. To stop the motion sickness caused by the rollercoaster ride of emotions. I know this has been my experience too. I was telling a friend that for years I seemed to have reoccurring melancholic moods, with a touch of anxiousness, most certainly just after my birthday in October through to the New Year, and other distinct times of the year as well. He suggested I might have Seasonal Affective Disorder (SAD) and that I should see a doctor. An "A-ha" moment! I went to my medical professional and talked things out with her. Because I still suffered from ongoing pain since after my surgery two years prior, she suggested a low-dose prescription for my depression that might also offer some help with my physical pains. I had tailbone pain, low back pain, knee pain, ankle pain. It always seemed to be something every day, and I felt like I was never getting any relief. I was tired of it all. Unfortunately, after a month on this particular medication, I emotionally felt a little "funny," but I figured that was part of taking new medication.

A month later, I was planning my death. Again. I remember going to a vision board party with some friends. I was thinking how badly I *needed* to go to the party because I knew I had the sense of not really knowing who I was and what was going on in my life. I had a breakup with a boyfriend. My father was in the hospital. I felt like I didn't know what to do with my life. I really needed to go to the vision party. I put together a vision of what I wanted for the new year, and for the rest of my life, and I *thought* I was good. But I didn't *feel* it. Something drastically changed the next day. I was triggered by a thought, which escapes me at the time of this writing, but I remember what emotions the thought caused. A chain of other thoughts had me spiraling into the dark abyss of depression. My old dark friend was waiting for me. I was supposed to go to an annual family Christmas party, where my extended family would be. It was an annual event that I used to be so fond of. I should have been preparing to socialize, play games, and exchange gifts. Instead, I sat at my dining room table, caught up in the cascade of different thoughts, one after another, thinking to myself, one solemn breath at a time: *I. Just. Can't. Do. This.* I just can't go. I can't move forward. I can't move backward. I was stuck in this loop of thinking. Sometimes our heart can be paralyzed, making it nearly impossible to think the right thoughts (Cady, 1896). I was riddled with fear too. What was I going to do?

Humiliation

My son, God bless him, was wondering what was wrong. We talked about bringing his best friend to our family's Christmas party, or just having my son go hang out at his friend's house. I decided that I just couldn't do life anymore. I needed to get my son to safety. So, I decided not to go to my family's event. Rather, I didn't really think about not going; I planned on ending my life. I walked to the car and told my son I was going to drive him to his friend's house. Though it was freezing cold outside, I didn't put a coat on. It didn't matter. I don't even remember if I had my keys. I do remember my son carrying my purse for me. I was in a state of a fog. My 15-year old son knew something was wrong. We got into the car. I didn't put on my seatbelt. I figured maybe that was one way I could end it. I dropped my son off, and unbeknownst to him as I watched him walk into his friend's house, I said goodbye to him, thinking for the last time.

I cried because I love my son. Sometimes I felt like I was not strong enough to be there for him and be the type of mother he needs. I considered driving myself straight to a psychiatric hospital, knowing I was in crisis and that I needed someone to be able to help me. But I didn't want my family to know. "Humiliation, worrying about what others think and displays of anger or shouting are areas of deep concern for the intuitive-sensitive person working out their level of sensitivity. It also impacts in terms of their deepest fear: humiliation" (Sawyer, 2015). Two years later, I was diagnosed with Bipolar Type II. Having a professional articulate and diagnose what I was experiencing for decades felt, in many ways, freeing.

However, it was embarrassing to tell my family and friends that I struggled for years and that I needed help. Oftentimes, I was indeed feeling great. Feeling like I had a life of purpose, excited about all the inspired ideas in my head, and positive that I was going to make a difference in the world. Then there would suddenly be times when that was not the case. I felt depressed, alone, and a failure. Nothing really mattered anymore. I ensured that I acted as happy and positive as I could while putting on a mask so that I didn't share what was going on—until I'd hit breaking points. Thankfully, I see the big picture now. I still struggle sometimes, yet I have a whole new perspective with a toolbox of complementary and traditional support strategies. When I think back, it makes me sad, yet I know when life is really, really good, I'll be able to look back at the sadness and see a difference. I'll always be able to treasure enjoying that difference.

I felt like a hypocrite, an imposter, because the concepts of Full Glass Living came to me about two years prior to the last crisis incident. So, how could I be this stress management coach, this emotional empowerment and wellness advocate, who is so good at encouraging and supporting others, yet not supporting myself? I had it all wrong. I don't have to be someone who has it all together all the time. I'm living a human existence right now. It took the last year of finishing this book for me to realize that. A lot of other people are hurting. Maybe you're reading this, and you're hurting right now. Just know that you're not alone. It's okay to cry. It's okay to be mad, sad, or afraid. Perhaps even afraid of what you are feeling. However, the biggest thing you must promise yourself is to reach out to those who can help. If you don't have a tight-knit circle of family and friends to reach out to immediately, you could always reach out to various centers or therapists. It's important to know that clinical depression, or any other mood disorder, needs to be assessed by a qualified health professional. There's even a hotline you can call.

Having depression, anxiety, or any mood disorder really sucks. One of the most frustrating things I hear when I tell a family member or friend that I'm feeling off, is getting the question, "What's wrong?" It's like they don't understand that there really doesn't have to be anything wrong. It's just the sense that there is no hope, and not having hope. It's almost like there's one side of my brain saying, *Remember that God loves me and God loves you.* That's what the Full Glass Living concept is all about. Whereas on the other side, I look at the glass as if nothing is there. It's a strange reality. I even felt like I was a poor example of a woman of faith. However, it is noted that many people of the Bible struggled with depression (Green/Longman, 1996).

If you or someone you know needs extra support or is in a crisis, please contact:
Suicide Prevention Hotline
1-800-273-8255
suicidepreventionlifeline.org

National Alliance of Mental Illness Crisis Text Line
Text NAMI to 741-741
nami.org

I Don't Know About You, But My Glass Looks Half-Empty

To write this book, I had to overcome the pessimistic and disempowering belief of the glass as half-empty...that something was missing. Sometimes, I felt overwhelmed, as if I were floating in this half-empty glass, sometimes drowning in it. If I could just get my head above water, I would be okay. My feelings would reside around pessimism, irritation, overwhelm, disappointment, discouragement, and definitely fear...all limiting beliefs about my existence. I would come up with excuses for why I couldn't do things, afford things, get out of debt, etc. How did a fairly optimistic girl turn so pessimistic as a woman? Has the proverbial cruel, hard world done it? Or was it just me tolerating limiting beliefs about myself and my life experience?

In this glass model, we can see some content in our life, yet we focus on what we *don't* have. We keep reaching for the seemingly empty space and dismiss the good that is in our lives now. I've been challenged with this, both in my emotional and material life. I grew up in a beautiful and loving home environment. I was blessed to be raised by both my parents through my years and spent countless family vacations, holidays, etc. with them. My great-aunt once called us the Brady Bunch because of how often we did things together. In fact, my younger sister, brother and I put on shows for my parents, most notably a "magic show" complete with an opening music act. We were a creative bunch of characters, and we loved each other and our extended family too.

With all this around me, I still struggled with my emotions and limiting beliefs. I was *different*. Physically, I was different because of a birthmark that I have on my chin. From my earliest recollection in grade school, I was teased incessantly about my birthmark. I would come home almost every day crying to my mother, saying, "the kids don't like me." She tried to console me time and time again with words of wisdom. Words I've given to my own son. *Don't worry about what others think. People can be cruel.* The most insulting comment I ever received from my parents was them saying, "You're beautiful." I didn't believe them because I chose to believe the words of my peers instead. I was too young and immature to understand social injustice and humanity's dark side. I didn't understand that there was no need to wrap myself up in what others thought of me in order to define who I truly was. Such a shame in some aspects, because that way of thinking for so many years, along with my artistic, intuitive, and emotional gifts, distorted the woman I would quickly grow up to be. It took a lot of personal development and self-awareness tools to see the light now.

Limiting Beliefs

Bruce Schneider, in his book *Energy Leadership: Transforming Your Workplace and Your Life,* explains that all limiting thoughts, emotions, and behaviors have energetic properties at the cellular level. These all can create blocks if they are negative ones.

The Four [Energy] Blocks are:

- The limiting beliefs that you hold
- The false assumptions from the past that you bring to today
- The false interpretations that you make
- The fear that you are not enough, the inner critic, or what is sometimes called a 'gremlin'

The Benefits of Pessimism and Needless Sacrifices

Being pessimistic has its benefits. We can be led into the thought of safety because there is no point in reaching outside of ourselves or reaching for the next possible level because things will work out. It can feel good, in a way, to complain and explain our way back to the woe-is-me attitude. I even adopted a sacrificial lamb belief that coyly looked like servant leadership. "Why are you trying to be a martyr?" my friend Leo once asked me at work. I was a needless martyr. The worst type of all, because at least a martyr was fighting and championing a cause that was *also* representative of themselves and who they truly were and believed. Jesus, Martin Luther King, and Gandhi were all about putting their life on the line because they knew it was the right thing to do, and they were ordained and guided by God to do so. But me? At various jobs, I was putting my life on the line, risking rest and my own physical and mental health because someone needed a favor, caffeinated or decaffeinated coffee, or insurance paperwork completed...now! It was about putting my needs on the back burner because you deserved it, and I didn't. You need to have this, but I don't deserve to have the same. You want something? Tell me what it is, and I'll go find it, steal it or whatever I have to do to get it for you. Me? Oh, no, thank you. I'm just fine. I don't need to have anything. Why could I not just allow myself to receive all the goodness that was coming my way? Why would I self-sabotage and thwart the goodness? Creating excuses for why I didn't deserve it?

Gratitude

When we see the glass as half-empty, there's usually that person who says to you in an ever-so-cheerful voice, "Well, you know you just have to look on the bright side!" *Insert internal eye roll. Please shut up.* This can be easier said than done. Let me stay in my dismay. It actually feels good to blame. Blame others. Blame the situation. Blame myself. What I can or cannot be, do, or have. We sometimes like to tumble down the woe-is-me staircase, feeling as if falling flat on our face is deserving and that anyone who says otherwise is disillusioned. Yet, there truly is something to acknowledging that there is ALWAYS some thing to be grateful for. When you are sliding down the rails and hoping that you don't crush your family jewels as you approach the end of the banister on the way down, you can make very small, extremely minute awareness of appreciation. Well, hmm. At least I don't have to walk down the stairs. At least I know that this ride will end at some point. At least I know that there are a certain number of steps on this staircase. I jest. But it really does work. I'm financially strapped for cash. At least I know where I stand with my finances. At least I know that I need to ask for help. From there, we begin to strengthen our gratitude muscle. It's an exercise for dumping the beliefs that hold you back, and becomes a clearing for the mind, body, and spirit. If you fail to exercise your gratitude muscle, you will have atrophy and lack the power and strength to use it again when you really need to. So, taking a look again:

Finances

- At least I know where I stand with my finances and I know that others have been in my situation.
- At least I know that there are ways people have gotten help.
- At least I know that people have had success in increasing their cash flow and net worth.

Love and Caring

- At least I know that I care about something.
- At least I know that I care.
- At least I know that others may care.
- At least I know that someone may be thinking about me, even the stranger who notices that I exist.

The Environment

- At least I know that the pouring rain covers everyone.
- At least I know that we need the rain.
- At least I know that life can't exist without the rain.

Thoughts & Feelings

- At least I know that I exist.
- At least I know that I matter.
- At least I know that I care enough to even go through this process, as dumb as it seems.
- At least I know that I have my own thoughts.
- At least I know that I can think.
- At least I know what I know.

Specific Possession

- At least I know that I have a car and it gets me where I need to go.
- At least I know that I appreciate my car.
- I appreciate that I can drive.
- I'm in gratitude that I can drive my car, and no one has to do it for me.

This can continue until you are able to take notice of other things. Again, we can build on the gratitude muscle. But it takes one baby step at a time. The tremendous thing about gratitude is that once we start acknowledging and being grateful for the simple things, it's almost like magic! We let go of the stress and worry and other limiting beliefs, even if it's just for a little while, and we begin to see more. We begin to receive more! God gives us more once we prove that we can handle what is going on right now. I would not give a student a saw to cut wood if they have not learned and appreciated how to hold a butter knife to cut bread. I like how Rick Warren in his book, *The Purpose Driven Life: What on Earth am I Here For?*, shares that we reinforce what God has in store for us when we take time to take note and keep a spiritual journal. This is an excellent way for us to record with gratitude.

I See the Half-Full Side of Things

Ah! Positivity! I see that I have flowers and a home, and all the stuff that life is about, right? The glass is half-full. I look and appreciate my career, home, family, and friends. I reach for the rainbow, and if it's just out of reach, I say, "That's okay." This is not a *bad* place to be. It is certainly more livable. However, the cloud of "what if" lingers in the back of the mind. A whisper from God saying: *You can see and do better. I did not make you to be mediocre, but to shine and be an example of my greatness.* We can have feelings of optimism and contentment, but also sense that we may be missing a key component to our life. What else is there? Should I be satisfied with what I have? Am I asking for too much, more than my share? My core positive beliefs assured me that I was well taken care of, and I was happy for what I have, but there was something more...

Positive Thinking as a Manifestation

"For as he thinks in his heart, so is he." (Proverbs 23:7, NKJV)

As we will examine further in the next chapter, we can co-create what shows up in our life. For now, let's look at how this applies to the glass half-full model. Our thoughts can create what we see—our perception. They have the power to shift our mood and actions.

Thoughts - Feelings - Actions = Results (Feedback-Adjustment Loop)

It is amazing how we can create a new life story, those things from the past even, just by adjusting our thoughts and beliefs, feelings, and moving-forward actions to obtain new results in our life. Indeed, some of the life experiences I had, in reflection now, moved me forward to the next level of my game. I was thinking in a limited way years ago about a situation. Now that I look at that same situation, I have new thoughts and feelings that have set me in a different trajectory.

Handling Life's Storms

When it rains, it sometimes is accompanied by storms. One year, I had two uncles die, then my grandma and great-aunt were diagnosed with cancer. My emotional health was a wreck, my son wasn't doing well in school, I couldn't lose weight, and my love life was a mess. Thinking about life's weather-related storms also allowed me to reflect on the other storms we deal with in our life. Those storms that impact us mentally, emotionally, financially, and spiritually can shift our positive attitude if we're not careful. Thinking with the glass half-full allows us to be better equipped to handle life's ups and downs. Interestingly, what experts say we should do to prepare for weather-related storms seems to apply with personal-life storms too:

- **See the signs & prepare:** If we pay attention, we get warnings to course-correct in our daily life. Sometimes we see the storm increasingly brewing, and we can make intentional preparations.
- **Respond**: Whether we could see the signs, or the storm came out of nowhere, it's our response to handling life's challenges that will make a big difference!

- **Ride it out:** Sometimes, it makes sense to "ride out" the storm because we saw the signs, made preparations, and have Rock Solid Faith that "this too shall pass."
- **Seek Help & Evacuate:** In other times, we need to use that Rock-Solid Faith and seek the paths of help that have been given to us and evacuate the situation.
- **Assess any Damage:** We then can assess the new situation after the storm, take in our new realities, and stabilize our energies.

If you're going through a storm, may you find peace in the midst of it and blessings in the aftermath! When I balance myself out in the aftermath, I pull out all the stops. Prayerful gratitude, mindset shifts, denials, affirmations, professional therapy, and coaching (yes, life coaches have coaches), mindful movement, aromatherapy, and any other complementary therapies I can get my hands on. A return to homeostasis.

Getting Hacked and Other Life Attacks

Another test of having a positive attitude is when your vulnerability is affected. I've had my account hacked, at least twice. I've had to say prayers of blessing for the perpetrators. I'm saddened that they were stuck in the limiting belief that in order to get ahead in life and get theirs, they needed to take that which did not belong to them. I'm sure they believed that they had a legitimate reason. How far do we think keeping a scarcity mindset is going to take us? And sheesh...did they really have to use the tactic of spammy deceit to get ahead? (as if ANY deceit is okay, really...). Well, I'm not buying it! As we'll discuss in the next chapter, we have the opportunity to rest that the Most High is unlimited. First, believe that the Glass is ALWAYS full, then you will see your good. I wonder, what lesson reminders could I draw from the violation?

My Cup is Full and Runneth Over

In seeing the glass as always full, what I like to call Full Glass Living, we create a more enlightened perception of our lives. We see that no matter how much "water" is in the glass, the glass is indeed always full. It is knowing that Divine Love "has your back always" and we appreciate ALL that is there to support our fulfilling life. In her book, *I Should be Happy But I'm Not: The 6 Practices of Emotionally Fit people*, Heidi Di Santo (2015) says, "Regardless of whether you judge the circumstances of your life as good or bad, your life has been perfectly constructed so that you can learn from your journey and fulfill your life's purpose."

Let me explain. We can get caught up in the "stuff" of what is in the water. Money, career, to-do lists, goals, achievements, but in another perspective, spiritually, we are attached to the other things, which may appear like empty space that is ever-present in our lives. We can develop the supportive beliefs that we have everything we need always, whenever we need it. Love, freedom, appreciation, passion, happiness, and gratitude are omnipresent because He is. In referring once again to Margaret Wheatley, she explains that: "Space is never empty. If it is filled with harmonious voices, a song arises that is strong and potent." God is never empty. Therefore, when I create goals from this perspective, I harness the emotions and beliefs that I am only manifesting into physical form what I already have. The positive beliefs and emotions...all of them are needed and are part of this creation process.

Sense of Awe

Have you ever felt what it's like to sit in the ray of sunshine and feel that all is well? It is a delicious feeling. No worries. No dreams or hopes lost. Goodness is all around. It is simply sheer bliss. I believe it's because we allow ourselves to stop chasing the doing and settle into being. It also opens the gates to recommit to what is important. From there, we find a new sense of awe about what we are capable of and able to take action on these commitments.

John Maxwell says, "Once we make a commitment, the resources follow, but they seldom follow until we declare our commitment. From the text [Daniel 3:1-18], we learn the following about developing commitment:

1. It usually begins with a struggle.
2. It seldom surrounds abilities or gifts.
3. It is the result of choice, not condition.
4. It is fostered when we settle the issue before it arises.
5. It is enhanced by deep trust in God.
6. It lasts when we remain single-minded." (Maxwell, 2007)

The Love You Deserve

I once asked a friend why I kept attracting men who were mentally, emotionally, physically, and, God help me, spiritually unavailable. He said that wasn't my issue. My issue was that I kept tolerating it. That I accepted less than standard, less than what I deserved in a relationship because I just wanted to have *something*. Something was better than nothing. My glass was half-full because of it. But if something is worth having, wouldn't we want it to be the *right* thing? Why would I tolerate what is not good for me? What is the fear of just waiting and knowing that the right person I deserved was waiting for me, and I needed to accept and receive that reality right now? I came to the resolution that I did have a relationship with a conscious, committed man; he hadn't revealed himself to me at the moment. Coming to terms with the seemingly empty space of my glass was paramount. My blessing was there; I just couldn't see it yet, but it did indeed exist.

Recognizing Answers to Prayers

Have you ever missed recognizing an answer to a prayer, well after it was presented to you? Well, I have! It's really funny how we can pray for a blessing, and when it shows up, we don't recognize it for what it is—on the spot. Then hours later, that blessing is like, "Smack! Hey, stupid, I'm still here waiting on YOU!" That's the whole premise of Full Glass Living—seeing the good that is always there. Ironically, in my own teaching of this work, a blessing escaped my conscious mind. My lapse in seeing my reality cost me frustration, agitation, and "hanger pangs" from skipping meals as I spent hours trying to resolve a challenge instead of relaxing into the answer that was given to me...hours ago. At the time, I was in bankruptcy and trying to sort the new bills that were coming in the mail for medical support for me and my son. I was swamped, then swamped some more. I was so mentally spent on sorting it all out that I had to pull out all my emotional support tools to unwind, including rubbing an aromatherapy tension blend on my temples and taking a mental break on the sofa. Then, "Smack!" An epiphany. The realization that the simple answer to my prayer was right there! I couldn't see it because I was bent on seeing things in a narrower context. Thank goodness that Divine Love is patient with us!! It's like sitting at the finest restaurant and wanting more water, but shooing the server away when he offers more. It's like sitting at the table at home, hoping to get more water to quench your thirst. The pitcher is right there on the table, but you refuse to take it and pour.

I'm so grateful that there is a built-in reset button. As magnificent as God wants us to be, I think it was clear that we were going to fail miserably on many pursuits, even fall completely off the track or go backward! Hence, Divine Intelligence designed the reset button. Maybe that was the plan all along? There are plenty of cool lessons that can only be gained from setbacks and failures. I can get myself hung up on doing things "right." If I fail or don't live up to my expectations, I've tossed in the towel and told myself what an idiot I am. I'm remembering more and more that in this human experience, there is beauty in the reset. This ability to start new is inspiring.

Prayer and Meditation

Prayer is a petition to Divine Love, while meditation is the listening and hearing in the heart. The Bible says that we should pray incessantly and equally, allowing the meditation of our heart to be received. For prayer, I know as you read this, you may be thinking, *Well, how is she going to tell me how to pray when she doesn't know my religious or faith background?* Like all the other suggestions for relieving limiting beliefs and emotions, such as stress, worry, and fear, I suggest you create your own system. However, I believe that even atheists can pray. If you understand that there is a science to how the world works, there are physical aspects to life, then you can pray to what it is you thought that may attempt to distract you away.

Do not judge this process, either. In meditating on the Word, you can become distracted. Lovingly acknowledge it and move back through the process of noticing what is. In time, you will find the sweetness of good, and the answers come forth from Him. There is nothing to do in these moments. After your meditation time, you can jot down any thoughts, A-has, or feelings you have from the process. Sometimes Divine Inspiration and God's words will come straight to you. Other times you may conclude your prayer and meditation feeling like you did a shoddy practice, then have a spark of inspiration later in the day or even the week. I believe it's because you allowed yourself to stop chasing the doing and settle into your being.

Putting a Cap on God's Blessings

Sometimes I had put a cap on my blessings. I was thinking it was not acceptable to receive. What did I think was going to happen if I let the goodness come my way? Would I not know what to do with it? Did I think it was going to be taken away? I also believed that others could have it, but for some reason, there wasn't enough for me that I missed the boat, and there was no need to try to achieve building my business, getting financially free, or even writing this book. Others have been there and done that, but there was no way I could have the same dreams come true. There wasn't enough substance, support, or success to go around. I remembered to be honest, repeatedly reminding myself that God, the Great I AM, the Universal, is abundant. This is a hard concept to wrap one's head around. If the Great I AM is ever-present and there were no limits, then there is no scarcity. I'm a daughter of Divine Life. You're a child of Divine Life. Why should we limit the unlimited? Why think in lack when we can think of unfailing abundance? We all can have what we want in alignment with the Great I AM, the Omniscient. We run around, trying to get to be the first, without realizing that we can get there safely.

I see this every day while driving my car on the highway. People will zip in and out of traffic, just to be first at the red light. Perhaps they're racing to change from Clark Kent to Superman to save the day. Perhaps they're racing to the hospital to be next to a loved one in critical care. If so, God bless them. For many, it is all about having first dibs at whatever "it" is to have, defined as the substance of our desires. So we think we desire. We can't patiently wait our turn knowing that we ALL can have it with a higher level of realization. In fact, we can all have it at the same time. So, what was my problem? I would think that there was not enough. Not enough money, not enough time. Indeed, I was not enough. In the book, *The Abundance Book*, John Randolph Price

(1987) says, "… Spirit within you is forever thinking thoughts of abundance, which is its true nature…Your Self thinks, sees, and knows only abundance; and the creative energy of this Mind-of-Abundance is eternally flowing, radiating, expressing, and seeking to appear as abundance on the physical plane." In the Full Glass concept, we look at our entire good of abundance as components of The Glass, The Water, and The Pitcher. Let's go to the next chapter to take a look!

CHAPTER 2

The Glass

Be the Sparkling Glass

L et's begin by looking at the fact that there is so much more going on than just the water in your glass. I need you to take the time and be aware that there is The Glass, which represents YOU—the real you. There is also The Water which represents all the stuff, the activity in your life. Finally, there is The Pitcher, the Infinite Source of all that you need to sustain life.

The Capacity to Hold

As mentioned before, The Glass is you—the real you. It starts with the energetic spiritual being that is you. In combination with the thoughts and feelings that you experience, which are only extensions, making up the total you...The Glass. As no two people are exactly alike, the same can be said about your glass. Most of the time, the metaphor for the glass half-empty, half-full question shows a tumbler. I want you to consider the look, shape, and color of your glass. Is it a sturdy tumbler, a refined wine glass, a decorative bowled glass? Is it small or large? Is it clear or colored? How would you describe the container base/foot, sides, bowl or stem?

If you describe yourself as a shot glass, this means that the capacity for what you can hold in your life *right now* will have less volume than say a large 20 oz tumbler. And that is okay. I want you to recognize this because it means so much to what I want you to consider as we move forward in coming to terms and work to dump your limiting beliefs and looking at *your* glass as always full. When our capacity to hold is taken care of, we are better equipped to hold more of the figurative water. We can fill ourselves up with the goals, tasks, and wants, tangible or intangible, that fill up our days.

For many people, including yours truly, accepting your current glass container can be difficult. Oftentimes we can go through life wanting to take the shape of someone else's glass. My friend Mary, and sister in Christ, is like a solid, sturdy glass ready to take on the world with fever. Yet I'm not her, and I shouldn't strive to be like her glass. I'm not saying that you can't trade-in or upgrade your glass. That is part of the human experience that when we get out of our comfort zone, we upgrade our glass. However, there is a false sense of life when we don't first accept and embrace our own capacity as it is now. The wonderful news is that, as we learn and grow and develop ourselves, our capacity to hold <u>more</u> is made available! That is when we're ready for the next glass upgrade.

Taking Care of Your Glass - Clean It

Jesus said, "First make the inside of the cup clean, and then the outside of the cup can be truly clean." (Matthew 23:26 NCV). Your glass is strong, yet fragile. Without care, it can break and crack. It is so important to care for it, wash it completely from time to time, and polish it to a healthy shine. The magic happens when you find ways to strengthen your glass through intellectual, emotional, physical, and spiritual growth. Really consider this concept. What are the activities that can expand your growth in each of these areas? This is how you ensure your glass is sturdy, brilliant, and ready to hold all the water you want in your life.

CHAPTER 3

The Water

Pour the Water

Next in our examination of the Full Glass concept is that of The Water in our glass. Water is literally the stuff life is made of. Water gives and helps create life. It includes those things that we want in our life, the things that we do, and the things that we want to enjoy. We must be clear about what we think and do, as it can get the best of us. At one point in my life, a dear friend of mine called me the "Committee Queen." I had a lot on my schedule. I was my son's Cub Scout den leader, an officer with my local Toastmasters club, worked full time, was starting my own business, and still tried to fill in the gaps with other activities. He didn't understand how I was doing it all, and oftentimes, I didn't either.

Here's the thing, there is a difference between being busy and being productive. Yes, I was doing a lot of activities, but I was productive because I could see the benefits it had for myself and others and the objectives that I cared about. The missing pieces were how I used the gaps or spaces of time, so I didn't overdo it. Sometimes I tried to drink more than my fill.

Nerdy Science About Water

Water is active and reactive. Its active properties create the energy, enjoyment, and substance in our life. At the same time, it can be reactive, changing, and adaptive to the many facets of what life has to offer. One of the most important principles to understand in the Full Glass Living model is that a full glass includes the air inside the glass. If you recall from your primary school education, air consists of oxygen, nitrogen, and other gases, as well as water vapor. All these components are necessary to sustain life on Earth. Obviously, we breathe in air! We also learned about the science of condensation in grade school, a reaction when cold and hot air meet. Think about all the "hot air" going on with others that can condensate onto your glass. When we are under stress, it's this "hotter air" that we see on the outsides of our glass. What we missed in the glass half-full/half-empty metaphor is that we need that open space. It allows us the quiet, peace, and reflection necessary to grow as human beings and accept that all is provided—always.

What am I Supposed to be Doing?

In the recent few decades, I was confused about what the heck I was supposed to be doing with my life. What should I fill my glass up with? I fell into the hospitality industry after one unsatisfying term at college in my freshman year. I originally enrolled in interior design because during my childhood I was so good with the arts: drawing, painting, music, you name it! I also enjoyed rearranging my room a gazillion times, so choosing a career of studying the arts seemed like a natural choice. Then during my first term as a freshman, I didn't enjoy the program. I was getting C's for work that really wasn't that complicated and looked like everyone's work, in my humble opinion. I was no longer the art teacher's pet like in high school. So, I decided to take my thoughts about being an interior designer of hotels to working in a hotel. After college, I worked my way around the operations part of the hospitality industry, fell into human resources, then training, then was introduced to the world of public and motivational speaking, then teaching hospitality at a college to then thinking that I wanted to teach something else. I wanted to blend my experiences in hospitality and emotional sensitivity with my creative energy to start my own company with services in stress management. But what was that supposed to look like? What should I do to gain the experience? What the heck was I supposed to be doing?

Focus and a Cluttered Mind

How often do we try to operate with a cluttered mind? So many to-dos, responsibilities, goals, and ambitions. It can be like a kid in a candy store...finding it difficult to choose one thing to savor FIRST! Everything seems so inciting and warrants for our attention. For me, multi-tasking is overrated. I do it very well, and stuff gets done. However, I don't always get the rich depth and clarity that I yearn for. Plus, the energy of scatteredness usually leaves me feeling...off. Good Lord, my mind could go in different directions all at the same time! It is like a street intersection with red, yellow, and green lights that flick haphazardly with no rhythm, rhyme, or reason. Go; stop; no, wait; go; no, stop; stop; no, go. It slowed me down. It also scared the crap out of me because I couldn't get centered on my plan of action for building my business. I also got caught up in the activity of non-income-producing activities. I could easily get distracted following the next new shiny jewel that I could look at. It has taken lots of discipline to break down my goals and activities into manageable, realistic pieces of the whole. That's why having a planning system that aligns with what I truly want has been so critical to me. I would get so fearful of what was the "right" step. I would confer with friends and family on what I should do. Ask professionals. I didn't just shut up and ask my damn self what I wanted. I didn't always shut up, meditate, and ask God what He wanted me to do. When my friend Leo and I worked together, he as my then boss (which was a pain in the butt back then), one of the things he used to say all the time was "focus!" Well, how the heck was I supposed to do that when I had a gazillion things to do and had more tasks coming my way? More and more now, I interestingly had to practice focusing attention on one thing at a time. (My multi-sensory-seeking mind still fights me on this).

Defining Success

As we further look at the water in our life, we apply the concepts of success to it. How do you define success? Some will say it's when you make a lot of money or get a fabulous job. Maybe when you are a celebrity. Don't let others determine that for you. And they will try. I define success as setting out an aspiration or a goal and strategies to consider making it happen. Then it happens. I also stay open that my success may come in a form that was unexpected. Which is why again, I leave some of that seemingly empty space in my glass for that. You don't know all of the good the Divine Life has for you. If you cut Him off, you're cutting yourself short. It's in the eye of the Great Beholder.

Is Your Water C.L.E.A.R.?

When you observe the facets of your life, do you have full transparency of the situation? Can you see what the issue is? Or, do you have a cloudiness of judgment and perception? We can promote our water's fluidity, the ideas, activities, and goals you have that are not stuck or frozen. In financial terms, we even use the term "liquidity" as having immediate, easy access to your assets. How about the energetic properties of the water in our life? Energy equals power. Water has the potential to be a calm stillness, or a swirling, rolling force. There is power in either.

Depending on the activity, you'll need the right type of energy. As in life, water has endless purposes. It's used for cleaning, washing, drinking, bathing, preparing food, nourishing plants in gardens, etc. Can the thought patterns and activities in our life be adaptable depending on life circumstances that come our way? Also, stagnant water gets filthy, bug-infested, and not suitable for drinking quickly. From time to time, your water needs to be reenergized and rejuvenated. It needs an upgrade in freshness so that life tastes a little better until the last sip! In summary, then, pouring C.L.E.A.R. water daily is a must:

o **Clarity** – Is your thinking about your life transparent or cloudy? What is it that you want most in your life?

o **Liquidity** – Are you frozen in your thoughts on how to obtain your goals? Or, are you open to inspiration?

o **Energy** – What shift in energy do you need in your thoughts? Do you need to calm down or open the flood gates to let new thoughts roll in?

o **Adaptability** – How can you allow your thoughts to adapt to the various circumstances in your life?

o **Refreshed** – Refresh your thinking by focusing on your new thoughts or affirmations.

CHAPTER 4

The Pitcher

"Some persons are like fish in the sea, saying, 'Where is the water?' In the presence of spiritual abundance, they cry, 'Where will I get the money? How will I pay my bills? Will we have food or clothes or the necessities?' Plenty is here, all around, and when you have opened your eyes of Spirit in yourself, you will see it and rejoice." - Charles Fillmore, *Prosperity*

Receive from The Pitcher

My hardest lesson has been on waiting and receiving. I can be so impatient. I want to reach my goals NOW! I want to lose 60 lbs. NOW! I want to write and publish my book NOW! For some silly reason, I've been very good at coaching my clients and students about the Law of Process. Things come in incremental "wins." It just looks like it comes overnight. However, it is a lesson that calls for patience, tenacity, and working towards goals. Keeping your eyes on the prize!

What has been even more difficult is for me to not get caught up in the "what I don't have" and the "I don't have enough" syndrome. Gosh, I was the poster child for "not enough." It ran as a theme of my self-worth *and* net-worth. I would forget that God's Abundance is always around us. This can be a hard concept to grasp if you are struggling to pay the bills. Trust me, I get that too. I constantly have to remind myself that there is always more than what is around. I just need to appreciate it. I'm a big fan of the business coach, Tiffany Peterson, who offered a challenge. It was to consider looking for all the pennies and feathers that show up in your world. They become the symbols of the abundance that is always around us. God supplies. Now you may be thinking, *pennies? Really?* Get excited about seeing pennies on the ground! You are attracting them, and they are waiting for you to receive! If you're not grateful for the pennies (which do add up, by the way), how will you be open to God's Abundance blessing you with more? Appreciate what you have. Sustain the capacity to pour and receive more.

Co-Create

When I worked at one hotel, I got introduced to Stephen R. Covey's 7 *Habits of Highly Effective People*. All the managers of the hotel went through a full two-day training on the topic. I loved it. It gave me a structured and centered way of approaching and organizing my ideas and life. I love how it helped me keep order and arrange the goals and things I want to accomplish. Recently, I found a daily planner that is more than a planner. It helped me understand what my life goals were. What did I want to be, do, and have? How could I break these down to life goals, year goals, then monthly, weekly, and day goals? Indeed, this book would not have been completed if it were not for me digging in, really getting centered about what I wanted in my life, praying and meditating on it, then organizing a structure for how I wanted to achieve them...with a space for flexibility, because God has humor and the human mind has its flaws.

If we lived our lives running around and trying to do what others want from us, we would feel out of use. Our life force would be sucked out, and we'd lie on our death beds, realizing that we never lived for ourselves. The only expectation I want to live for is the expectation from God. And I believe even Divine Love wants us to co-create that with Him when we get clear and align our free will with His will. So, in managing our time, why would we fill up our calendars with activities that do not bring these ideas to fruition? Procrastination is a form of fear. If I decided to do the laundry, run some meaningless errands for the day, and make excuses for the activity that really doesn't need to happen as a top burning priority TODAY, it keeps me safe from doing the big, hairy stuff like writing a book, teaching a meditation class, or giving a call to a business contact and asking for a deal. Managing our time is more than writing items in the day's calendar with the hours we want to do them. It's about being clear of what we want and looking for ways to make that happen.

Finding Peace in Spirit

In what ways do we fill up our spirit and ensure that we connect our souls to our higher power? We have the opportunity to remind ourselves over and over again that Divine Life lives in every cell and atom of our being (Hausmann, 2010). Yet, humankind seems to disconnect and struggle, recycling turmoil for centuries. What if each one of us took personal responsibility for our own inner peace? As the song goes, "Let there be peace on Earth and let it begin with me!" How do we cultivate and focus on peace during chaos? I do believe it is a choice, seemingly a difficult one, to focus on peace. There is so much out there constantly trying to grab our attention and destroy us. Let's practice more awareness back to The Good. For me, practicing this creates a sense of knowing Peace. It's ceaseless, along with prayers. Never stops.

Energy You Share in Other Capacities

I know I can get exhausted quickly. I don't know why: If it's part of an emotional disorder or how I'm wired. For years, I didn't realize this. I worked myself like a dog, buried in workaholism, then wondered why I didn't have the energy and would burn out. I'm like the energizer bunny that has a short-lived battery life. I can be a massive flurry of activities and accomplishments on my to-do list...you can't stop me. Until I realize that I must stop. I must refresh myself. Refill my glass, get some clean, clear water, and allow myself some self-care and good ol'-fashioned nothingness. Time to sit my butt down and do some work on doing nothing. This is also important not only for myself but for the benefit of others. I learned that effectively giving of one's time in paid or volunteer work is near impossible if you're too tired to provide it.

Affirmations & Denials

At my church and the faith-based perspective of Unity, I was reminded of the practice of affirmations and denials. As stated before, Jesus taught us the importance of cleaning the cup and the plate. He rebuked the error thinking (denial) and affirmed that which is Truth, which is of God. We can do this, too, by dumping the limiting beliefs and thinking that bind us. We will practice this in our day-to-day activities in the remaining parts of this book. Each day will cover a limiting belief, then we will dump it for a supportive, affirming process towards our good. You can also find more affirmations and other free resources at **fullglassliving.com**.

The Next Steps

Now it's time to apply the concepts of Full Glass Living in the *28 Days to Dump Limiting Beliefs* plan. Each day you will read the limiting "belief of the day," with a supporting story to challenge that belief. Afterward you will find C.L.E.A.R. questions, denials and affirmations, and tasks to clean out those old beliefs and pour in an enlightened sense of self, thereby increasing your capacity to appreciate Divine Mind within you.

PART II

Spirituality

DAY 1

I Don't Deserve to Be Happy

"Those people who know they have great spiritual needs are happy because the kingdom of heaven belongs to them." - Matthew 5:3 NCV

With my history of ups and downs in my emotional sensitivity, I began to wonder if I'd ever be happy. *Is anyone happy?* Just when I felt I would find my stride, I would feel the ping of negative emotional thinking or a full-blown breakdown. I started assuming that if I'm not happy, it's because I didn't deserve to be. How could I be happy if I have done so much wrong and failed so many times in "keeping it together?" I wanted to reach out to God for support and guidance but questioned, *Who am I to ask?* As a parent, I can appreciate the numerous times that I was disappointed in my son's choices. However, that never took away from the love I had for him. I was once reminded that God wants us to have a happy, joyful, prosperous life. So, why should we condemn ourselves not to follow His lead?

Full Glass Practice

- **C.L.E.A.R. Question** – What is your definition of happiness?
- **Denial** – *I dismiss the thinking that my Father does not love me.*
- **Affirmation** – *I am a child of God and accept myself unconditionally.*
- **Action for the Day**
  - Sit in gratitude for the care that Divine Love has for our life. He wants us to be happy.

DAY 2

I Need to Know All the Answers

"Trust in the Lord with all your heart, and don't depend on your own understanding;" - Proverbs 3:5 NCV

When I was a child, I always had a fear of death. I would go to sleep all comfy and rested for a night's sleep. Then the thoughts would flood in. What if I don't wake up in the morning? As the prayer goes, what exactly does "I pray the Lord my soul to keep" really mean? I would jump out of bed, panicked, pleading to God to rest my uneasy mind. What was eternity, and if there wasn't an eternity, then things will just end after we die? Just end! I was so fearful of either predicament because I needed to know the right answers and understand them. It would take a good 40 minutes to settle myself and relax.

When I was younger, my mother suggested that I attend my paternal grandmother's church, that perhaps having a more active Christian life would help me. It did for a while. Then over the decades, the midnight panic attacks would come again. I'd jump out of bed, plead to God to take away the fear, the chaos in my mind, the crazy hysteria. There was nothing that I could do about the predicament of death. As someone who likes to have control and understand what and when something is going to happen, that made me so fearful of death. Not accepting, but fearful. No matter how many times I could quote Bible verses or say my prayers, occasionally, I would swing back to those uncontrollable panics of worry. I had to get comfortable with the idea that some things I would not understand. My limited human mind couldn't comprehend. Releasing the need to be Ms. Know-It-All was in order.

Full Glass Practice

- **C.L.E.A.R. Question** - How have you blocked your peace because you needed to know all the answers?
- **Denial** - *I remove the distraction that clouds my vision of faith.*
- **Affirmation** - *I am open to the peace and understanding from God within.*
- **Action for the Day**
  o Ask a question that only Divine Love would have the answer to.
  o With loving joy and peace, take contentment that the answer may not be yours to know right now.

DAY 3

Divine Life is Punishing Me

"God sees me not as someone whose guilt calls for punishment, but as someone whose errors call for correction." - Marianne Williamson

deserved it. The mysterious monstrosity inside my chest that wanted to come out by no other means than surgery—I deserved it. I believed I had to own up to all my faults and flaws. The big blunders and the little ones too. The dark secrets that would remain within me to the grave. I had to repent *and* not receive grace. This was my punishment. Or, was it my awakening? I remember asking God, *Why is this happening to me?* Why did I have this aching pain that was now manifesting into something more major than I had originally thought? Why would I now have a scar prominently on my chest to remind me of what I had to go through? *It is because it will make you stronger and realize that I have a path for you.* Okay, Lord.

Sometimes the things that seem like punishments in our lives provide us with a chance for introspection. What we think is punishment from God may very well be the manifestation of our own error-thinking and choices. Our free will to create it.

Full Glass Practice

- **C.L.E.A.R. Question** - Now as an adult, if you were put in "time out" for error-thinking or behavior, how might that look?
- **Denial** - *Remaining in guilty thinking does not serve me.*
- **Affirmation** - *I profess my error-thinking and receive love and understanding.*
- **Action for the Day**
  o Reflect on a recent hardship (punishment) and find the lesson in it.
  o Write in a journal or notebook what insight you gained from acknowledgment.

DAY 4

I'm Failing at Being a Model of My Faith

"God has already taken into account the wrong turns, the mistakes of your life. Quit beating yourself up and accept His mercy." - Unknown

've been told time and time again that I'm "so sweet." I've been identified as wholesome, nice, respectable with conversation that includes the occasional "golly gee" or something to that effect. I'm a Christian, and I love my spiritual path and try to do and be the "right" thing. However, as God *is* my witness, He knows that I sometimes have a potty mouth. I'm putting myself out there to be vulnerable to the critics who might say, "whoa, Nelly, she's got a lot going on here." Yes, I do. I've got an open sweet spiritual mindset, ready to support, serve from a heart of gold. However, if I forget a task or drop something on my foot... let's just say I have a bit of swagger in my verbiage. In the past, this acknowledgment did not remove the limiting belief in my mind that I was a good Christian. I'm by no means princess perfect (who is really?), but perhaps as people compare their lives to those on social media, maybe I was doing the same with comparisons to my spiritual brothers and sisters?

Full Glass Practice

- **C.L.E.A.R. Question:** In what ways do you feel you are not a model of your faith or moral beliefs?
- **Denial** - *Berating my wrongs serves no purpose.*
- **Affirmation** - *I listen to the Still Small Voice and make course corrections along the way.*
- **Action for the Day**
  - Today, think of one adjustment in thought, feeling, or behavior that you can shift.

PART III

Self Esteem

DAY 5

I'm Not Smart Enough

"With the right mindset and the right teaching, people are capable of a lot more than we think." - Carol S. Dweck

When it was time for me to enroll in college, the university that I applied for accepted me under one condition. I had to attend their pre-freshman summer term in order to better prepare me for the rigors of academia. You see, I had good grades in high school. The problem was that my SAT scores were low. Complicated math and big words were not my strengths. The arts were. From there, I had set in my mind that I was not smart enough for many things. I mixed up my spelling; sometimes I'd jumble my words when I'm really excited to teach a topic. If someone used a word that I was unfamiliar with, I felt inferior. However, with the right steps and continued effort, I proved myself wrong. By surrounding myself with interesting ideas, books, online programs, and even teaching and coaching, I gained strength in being "smart" that I would have never gained had I stuck to my limiting belief about my capabilities. I also learned that everyone has their own combination of cognitive and emotional intelligence paths (see, I dropped some fancy knowledge on ya!). Many experts now agree IQ is not the be-all and end-all for measuring intelligence.

Full Glass Practice

- **C.L.E.A.R. Question** – What limiting beliefs do you have about your ability to think and feel?
- **Denial** – *Here and now, I remove the belief that there is only one measure of intelligence.*
- **Affirmation** – *I seek to be unified in Divine Intelligence every day.*
- **Action for the Day**
  o Take note of the type of activities that just "flow" from you without effort.
  o Do an online search for "multiple intelligences" and see what comes up for you.

DAY 6

What if They Laugh at Me?

"Love who and what you are and what you do. Laugh at yourself and at life, and nothing can touch you. It's all temporary anyway." - Louise Hay

Kids can be terrorizing little gremlins. Adults too. I have told my students that high school really doesn't end. The same ridiculing, bullying, in/out crowd mentality, and more show up in our adulthood, work, even in families. It's just more sophisticated and is called harassment, expectations, norms, and morals. It's normal to have the need to feel accepted on the playground instead of teased or laughed at. For those of us who struggle with being emotionally sensitive, this need and want can be especially hard for us. I hated being different. Something as simple as being born with a birthmark (like I can help that) made me feel different. I got teased repeatedly, seemingly every day of my grade school years. I was left with this shame of being who I was. It was shameful to simply exist. Those who struggle with being accepted for who they are: Black, Latino, White, Asian...

this list is not exhaustive. We all want to fit in. This shameful aspect of how I received the messages on the playground and how I internalized being fearful of who I was and wanting to hide or even fit in to be someone else was not healthy. Until I learned better. If God accepts me for who I am, how can I practice removing the dire need to be accepted by others?

Full Glass Practice

- **C.L.E.A.R. Question** – Have you ever felt like you didn't fit in? What beliefs did you accept that fueled the flame?
- **Denial** – *My worthiness and acceptance are not dependent on others.*
- **Affirmation** – *I deserve to be supported by those who care about me.*
- **Action for the Day**
  - Go watch a few online videos of Laughter Yoga clubs. You will see how people don't take themselves so seriously and actually laugh about things that normally would be considered very serious (disease, diagnosis, etc.).

DAY 7

I Will Fall Down

"A lot of people become discouraged too soon. The name of the game is that you got to be relentless." - Les Brown

One time in my school years, I literally fell. Really bad. I was new to my junior high track team. I was advised by other students that if you tell the coach that you'll do any track event, you would be put on the team. I obliged with the advice. After one practice, my coach informed me that I would train for hurdles. That sounded like fun! However, quickly I found that I really struggled with getting my legs properly over the hurdles. Shins and ankles were getting bruised.

Then came the fateful day on our first track meet when I was scheduled in the last heat to run hurdles. I got over the first hurdle, but the second one had something else in mind. I tripped and fell and slid on the hard, crumbled-gravel track surface. I looked up from lying on the ground, and while the other athlete finished her hurdles with her team cheering her on, my team stood in silence. They were obviously concerned about my welfare. I stood up, did my best to jump over the remaining hurdles, and even laughed at myself the rest of the way. My coach told me the next day that I had the heart; however, I was no longer going to be on the hurdle team.

How interesting it is to fall and expect that we will remain there. In most circumstances, we can get back up. Perhaps with gravel stuck down the long side of our legs, but we still get up to finish the race.

Full Glass Practice

- **C.L.E.A.R. Question** - When have you royally failed at something? Was it a public display of royally failing?
- **Denial** - *Failure is not the destination of my journey.*
- **Affirmation** - *My life lessons are found every time I get up and move forward.*
- **Action for the Day**
    o If possible, download a new game app or try a good old-fashioned table game with family or friends.
    o Notice how many failed tries or circumstances that come about. Try continuing the game to improve and move forward.

DAY 8

I Don't Think I'm Attractive Enough

"Self-acceptance and self-love are important but often misunderstood concepts these days. You should love yourself as a reflection of God's love and as someone put on this earth to make a unique contribution." - Nick Vujicic

A friend and I would love to go out to a club near our area. It's not that type of "club" full of partiers. In fact, the club is a really nice restaurant that has dancing in another section of the building. The atmosphere is fun, with a diversity of ethnicities and ages. It is a comfortable experience to hang out with her. Until...she gets asked out to the dance floor. The old feelings of rejection, ridicule, and the limiting belief that I'm not cute or sexy enough start flooding in. I worry about my weight instead of worrying about my mind and character. I worry about why someone didn't "choose" me, instead of being present to the joy my friend experiences on the dance floor. Even if I join my friend on the dance floor, I would be self-conscious about being seen. Strange, since I'm on "stage" for a living. However, being on stage and being on display are two different things. Having the power to push through this limiting belief takes a concerted effort and repeated practice. One of my favorite ways is through mirror work, introduced to me through an online program by the dearly departed Louise Hay (you will find her recipe for mirror work in today's action below). The practice offers self-acceptance and beauty of Self (with a capital S), inside and out.

Full Glass Practice

- **C.L.E.A.R. Question** – What is your definition of attractiveness?
- **Denial** – *My attractiveness is not set by human standards.*
- **Affirmation** – *I remain attractive by taking care of my spiritual, physical, and emotional needs.*
- **Action for the Day**
  o Stand in front of a mirror or have a small mirror in hand.
  o Look deeply into your eyes and repeat the simple phrase, "I love you. I really, really love you!"

PART IV

Health

DAY 9

What if Something is Wrong?

"We didn't need to change what was going on in our lives and surroundings so much as we needed to dig deeper and change what was going on within ourselves." - Mark Hyman

As an adult, it seemed I always had health issues going on. If it was flu season, I'd be the only one with the flu. Colds, sinus infections, ear-aches, joint pain, eczema, and other ailments were part of my seasonal experiences with my health. When I was introduced to functional medicine and holistic practices, I realized that there could be physical core causes of illness, as well as emotional. However, the biggest one of all? It was my *belief* that I would get sick! I would worry myself, almost to death, that something was wrong with me and that there was nothing I would be able to do about it.

Full Glass Practice

- **C.L.E.A.R. Question** – Can you recall a time when you probably manifested poor health into your life simply by thinking about it?
- **Denial** – *Worry about health and diagnosis is not in Divine Mind.*
- **Affirmation** – *I find resolve and peace with greater connection with my spiritual health.*
- **Action for the Day**
  - Go online and do a search for complementary therapies and holistic health practices.
  - Is there a new approach to your health that you can adopt starting today?

DAY 10

My Health Goal Will Never Work

"Whatever you're afraid to do but really want to do is exactly what you need to do." - Jessica Ortner

'm really going to try this again? I've tried losing weight so many times that I've lost track of the numerous programs. Every time I would start a program, I would do well. However, underneath it all, I had this limiting belief that it wasn't going to work in the end. Or maybe *I* wasn't going to work. Then there were the athletic goals of running a 5k or half-marathon again. With the creaky knees setting in and other bodily issues to complain about, I held on to the belief that I was just too old to attain the success in my health goals that I desired. I gave up before I even began!

Hence, the question, why would we assume that our health goals are not going to produce the results we want? Putting one foot in front of the other, checking off one step at a time is the way to reach success...even if we don't feel like doing it. The success we do achieve may not look exactly like we originally envisioned. It can be better because God directs our steps along the path.

Full Glass Practice

- **C.L.E.A.R. Question** - What are the major health goals you'd like to achieve this year?
- **Denial** - *I remove any limitations in my mind's eye on physical lack.*
- **Affirmation** - *I am joyfully alive, nourished, and evolving.*
- **Action for the Day**
  - Select one of your health goals and quickly do one thing that leans towards that goal.
  - Examples could be walking up the stairs twice, slicing an apple for a snack, taking a mental break, etc.

DAY 11

I Don't Think I'll Get Better

"A happy heart is like good medicine, but a broken spirit drains your strength." - Proverbs 17:22 NCV

After my surgery in 2014 to remove the hyperplasia of my thymus gland, there was much I couldn't do. Yes, I needed to take walks and breathe through a tube to expand the capacity of my lungs. But I couldn't drive, and I wasn't allowed to do push-ups. I had bread ties holding my rib cage together for goodness sakes! Just after surgery, my friend Mary said, "You know, you're going to have to let people help you." I was frightened by that concept. I was the one that was supposed to be doing the helping. How vulnerable and, dare I even say, embarrassing it was going to be to let someone else help me. God bless my mother, who probably did more than she really needed to bathe and take care of me. I was in despair. But among all that stress in recovery, the biggest issue I had was just Be-ing. Sitting in a chair or taking walks and realizing that it was time for me to look inward to take care of myself and just be.

Full Glass Practice

- **C.L.E.A.R. Question** – What does living in misery during illness or, living in gratitude through illness mean to you?
- **Denial** – *Ultimately, I am not bound by physical health.*
- **Affirmation** – *God's healing power is always at work in me.*
- **Action for the Day**
  o Take 10 minutes to build a self-care activity for tomorrow. Plan first thing in the morning to pray and meditate in gratitude for your healing.

DAY 12

Sleeping is for Lazy People

"[Sleep is]... a natural periodic state of rest for the mind and body. If you're not doing it, then you're being completely unnatural. And nobody likes unnatural people." - Shawn Stevenson

For the love of all that is good, please put your behind to bed. It is SO easy to get caught up in a Netflix binge because the series is so good. Believe me, I know. I've watched a whole season starting in the evening until the early morning, then went off to work. Did I feel like muck? Yes, indeed. Did I regret watching the show? Nope. What I didn't appreciate was the mind fog, impatience, and restlessness I had when I got home. I couldn't think straight and wanted to be left alone, let alone tackle any to-dos and issues that may have come my way. Having a consistent sleep ritual is important. Without it, the mind and body have a hard time understanding why you resist the natural rhythm of restorative sleep.

Our culture has perpetuated the idea that it is normal to

stay up super late, get up early, then down some coffee to get throughout the day. Then, we stay up late again because the coffee buzz hasn't worn off or we have just a few more episodes of that favorite TV show that will only be for "one hour"...turning into 2-3 hours. We think sleep is a luxury.

So, transitioning to a restful sleep allows our batteries to recharge. All the fear and anxiety of the day wreaks havoc on the quality of our sleep. Lying in bed, still thinking about our issues, doesn't help the problem. In fact, I've found that the wee hours of the night are when my stress and anxiety get turned up a notch. Probably because it's quiet, and I no longer have the distractions of ineffective busyness to cover my fear and worries of the day. I'm just lying in bed, and my mind and emotions decide it's now time to turn up the noise and have a fear and worry party! Letting go and succumbing to the delicious enjoyment of sleep adds years to your life. Seriously, it does and offers the chance to show up as the beautiful creature you are to be, do, and have more in your life.

Full Glass Practice

- **C.L.E.A.R. Question** – What are your beliefs about sleep? What is your usual routine for sleep?
- **Denial** – *Sleep is not a luxury only for those that have nothing to do.*
- **Affirmation** – *I ease into the peace that rest is required for my health and happiness.*
- **Action for the Day**
  o Try going to sleep 30 minutes before your normal sleep time.
  o Turn off the electronics 45 minutes before bed.
  o Create a bedtime ritual by diffusing some essential oils, close the blinds, put some soft music on, and sit in prayer and meditation.

PART V

Free Time

DAY 13

I Don't Have Enough Time

"All we have to decide is what to do with the time that is given to us." - J.R.R. Tolkien

Whenever a guru states that everyone is given the same 24 hours in the day, and creating a healthy, fulfilling lifestyle is a no brainer, I roll my eyes. Yes, we are all given the same 24 hours, but we are not given the same responsibilities and commitments. However, moving towards a lifestyle that we desire is possible when you have a plan. You will need a collection of strategies to release stress and enjoy that free time you deserve. Just as in your workday, no two days are the same, so can be the activities you engage in to release stress. Some strategies will work when you have a little more time on your hands; others are better on those long, grueling workdays. While other activities are perfect during periods of major projects or changes, others are excellent when you finally get some vacation time. The key to your plan is finding the segments of time you can utilize.

Full Glass Practice

- **C.L.E.A.R. Question** - What things gain your attention during most of the day? How have you put off taking care of your own needs because of it?
- **Denial** - *Time is limited in the construct of the human mind.*
- **Affirmation** - *I wisely dedicate my time to the commitments that are important to me.*
- **Action for the Day**
  - o If you don't have one, purchase a planner or use your phone app if that works.
  - o For today, schedule a 10-minute activity you can do for yourself.

DAY 14

I Don't Have Enough Energy

"The Lord is my shepherd; I have everything I need. He lets me rest in green pastures. He leads me to calm water." - Psalm 23:1-2 NCV

Getting comfortable with just doing nothing has always been a painful process. *What? Do nothing today? What a lazy you-know-what I would be!* There is always something to do! Always something that I can polish up and work on. But didn't God say let there be a day of rest? Wasn't He an advocate for taking rest breaks? So why damn myself by trying to be in a perpetual state of doing? Because I wanted to be a superwoman, supermom, super teacher, and super coach. I needed to prove to myself that my core being was defined by what I did. So, taking time to meditate? Why in the loony-tunes world would I do that? I could be doing something else. When I realized that deep prayer and meditation weren't just good for me but necessary as part of my spiritual-human experience, I understood that it was the core stuff of life's enjoyment. I could show up in the world as my true self. Ready and willing to be open to who I really was and to do and have what I really wanted and deserved. So, if the almighty God took a break, I totally must do it too! What I realized was the amazing way of restoring my energy. Instead of me griping about how tired I was all the time and that there was no time for me, I realized that joyfully scheduling that time for me was a beautiful thing.

So, I breathe, get quiet, and check into the miracle that I'm still alive, breathing. Just being in my own presence and with the presence of God. Jesus, my way-shower, who shows me the way to Full Glass Living, has said it in many ways. So, let me get to it! Let me sit my caboose on the sofa and stare at the wall, plant, or candle to unwind and restore my energy. (Let's not use that as procrastination, however). I can schedule the time to just be and enjoy some self-care; it makes a world of difference!

Full Glass Practice

- **C.L.E.A.R. Question** – Have you ever assessed why you might feel drained of energy? Can you identify your lifestyle choices that may contribute to it?
- **Denial** – *I remove the obstacles that drain my energy.*
- **Affirmation** – *I enjoy activities and interests that restore my mind, body, and spirit.*
- **Action for the Day**
  o Meditate. Yes, meditate.
  o Pick an affirmation, a scripture, or whatever feels comfortable to you, play soothing music in the background, and just be present to how you feel.
  o Notice any shifts in energy that the Holy Spirit provides you.

DAY 15

I Must Control This

"When your demons start to dance, remember you are
the DJ." - Robert M. Staples

had a habit of running away. Not from home, but from public
environments. There would be times when I was consumed
with a sense of dread and despair. This mix of panic attacks
and mood swings made me hypersensitive to not wanting to
make a spectacle of myself, and all I knew was that I needed to
get out. I'd flee to my car, usually driving somewhere to hide
from people. Even strangers. A random parking lot somewhere.
My boss, friends, or family would call to ask where I was, to offer
support, and beg me to come home. By then, I was numb. Too
numb to start the car back up. I wasn't going to drive home or
back to work, but I didn't want to remain in the obscure place of
controlled safety.

The most difficult part about this was the sense of being out
of control. I didn't realize how much I tried to control every
aspect of my life. How people accepted me, how I performed at
work, how other people performed at work. It was exhausting. I

realized that some things are purely out of my control. That there are times when I may need a little extra help and support.

Full Glass Practice

- **C.L.E.A.R. Question** - In what ways have you unrealistically tried to control others or yourself?
- **Denial** - *I release the false belief that to control means that I always know the outcome.*
- **Affirmation** - *I go with the flow and remain awake to what is presented to me.*
- **Action for the Day**
  - o Go for a walk, preferably in an area where there are parts of visible nature.
  - o Notice how the wind blows the trees or birds or squirrels move around. They do their will without your interference.

DAY 16

Taking Up a Hobby is a Waste of Time

"When we strip our lives of play and flow—as we so often do just to get everything done—our mood deteriorates." - Christine Carter

As I shared prior in this book, I was a very busy woman at one point in my life. Not to say that I'm not now. However, I neglected to place value in scheduling time for myself. Scheduling time for rest and relaxation, play, and doing something fun and creative. Since being a little girl, I've always loved the arts. Drawing, painting, crafts, music, dance...whatever! Again, I thought I would have a full-time career in art and design. Over the decades, it was as if I lost my way. I was no longer active in any of these pursuits.

Studies show that when people take the time to "turn off" and remove themselves from their day-to-day demands, they return to their commitments refreshed and enriched with vibrancy. Play is essential to a productive life.

Full Glass Practice

- **C.L.E.A.R. Question –** What hobbies or interests have you been attracted to that you put off being active in?
- **Denial –** *There is no reason to limit time to enjoy life.*
- **Affirmation –** *I enrich my life by creating time for fun and play.*
- **Action for the Day**
  - Practice mindful art. Grab a simple sheet of paper and doodle to your heart's content with every focus on each of the pencil strokes. Set your timer for seven minutes of play.
  - Take note of what it feels like to be in flow with free creative energy.

PART VI

Relationships

DAY 17

I'm Afraid to Be Alone

"My alone feels so good, I'll only have you if you're
sweeter than my solitude." - Warsan Shire

t took many years after my divorce, random dates, and, dare I
put into print, a consensual one-night stand, for me to realize
that I was really crapping out with my dating life. I vowed after
my divorce that I would never marry again, let alone change
my name. It's interesting how the thoughts we have manifest
into the experiences that we live. Then came the opportunity to
be involved with someone who provided what I needed most.
Attention. The sense of trust. I was just beginning to feel like I
would be alone until he came along. I feared that I would be at an
old age by myself, never finding my life partner, spending decades
of single night dates and singles' cruises and traveling.

Full Glass Practice

- **C.L.E.A.R. Question -** What does it feel like to enjoy
  your own company?

- **Denial** - *There is no limit to the love that can be found in many ways.*
- **Affirmation** - *The more I love myself, the more I can love others.*
- **Action for the Day**
  - Schedule some time this week to "do you." Go to see a movie, have dinner at a restaurant, anything that is typically done with others. (Do this even if you have a significant other).
  - Take note of what it feels like to enjoy your own company; offer unconditional love to yourself.

DAY 18

If I'm Honest, They'll Reject Me

"I've learned not to take people's 'No' personally. Some people will like what I have, and others won't. It's not my job to talk them into something they don't want." - Neal Anderson

Personally, I'm an honest person, but I hadn't been expressing my feelings or perspective with others. If it was something that needed to be stated that I thought would "hurt" the other person's feelings, I hesitated to share. I was afraid of being rejected. This occurred in all areas of my life with all sorts of relationships: professional, social, and within family. Unfortunately for my son, home life was the only area of my life where I spoke my opinionated truth. Raw, unfiltered opinion.

Is sharing one's own insight or opinion too wrong for me? I realized it stemmed from my own need to be accepted. I didn't want to be rejected, and in turn, I didn't want the other person to feel that I was rejecting them. What's curious was that I had been very good about coaching others through the process of firm, appropriate communication, but I hesitated in doing so in my own life for years.

Full Glass Practice

- **C.L.E.A.R. Question** - Have you held back in being honest about your thoughts and feelings with others?
- **Denial** - *My happiness is not contingent on others' yeses and noes.*
- **Affirmation** - *I radiate love and respect, and in return, I get love and respect.*
- **Action for the Day**
  o Think of an upcoming conversation and how you might state your truth in an honest and respectful way. This can be as simple as noting that you would prefer 10 minutes to yourself to unwind.

DAY 19

I'll Just Get Disappointed

"And patience produces character, and character produces hope. And this hope will never disappoint us because God has poured out His love to fill our hearts. He gave us His love through the Holy Spirit, whom God has given to us." - Romans 5:4-5 NCV

Maybe every parent goes through the same thing, but if I had a penny for every time I told my son to clean his room, I'd be an extremely rich woman. My son would seem disinterested, incapable, or suffers from an auditory-motor disability because it would take him months to completely get the job done. Months! The rest of our home was in fairly good shape, but his room? Good Lord, it was mess upon mess. Sometimes he would "clean" his room, which involved making a walking space from the front of his door to his bed. Not up to my standards.

I've found the same to happen in other relationship areas. When I decided to try online dating, I initially found myself setting up limiting beliefs about who I'd meet. He'll just dump me anyway. He's going to let me down; they always did. I had to catch myself and realize that although none of us are perfect, those who truly take a concerted effort deserves a chance. Also, what can I learn from all these experiences in feeling like others were letting me down?

Full Glass Practice

- **C.L.E.A.R. Question** - When has someone expressed that you did not meet their expectations, that you let them down?
- **Denial** - *I remove the need to control outcomes with factors I cannot control.*
- **Affirmation** - *I am open to the idea that the best attempts can create desirable effects.*
- **Action for the Day**
  o Think of someone whom you believe disappointed you.
  o Write a letter to them expressing the request for forgiveness and that you only wished you could learn from the action and/or be the person at that time capable of fulfilling their expectations.
  o Reverently throw the letter away.
  o Next, write a letter to God expressing how you want to be accepted in His sight for expectations and that we are all making the best attempt to do that for Him and each other. Tuck this letter in a place where you can refer to it at another time.

DAY 20

They'll Judge What I Think, Believe, or Do

"People will hate you, shut you out, insult you, and say you are evil because you follow the Son of Man. But when they do, you will be happy. Be joyful at that time, because you have a great reward waiting for you in heaven." - Luke 6:22-23 NCV

As mentioned prior, the desire to be accepted in my childhood also rolled into my adulthood. I increasingly realized that I had the unique gift of emotional sensitivity, to be able to support others who may be hurting. I also had the gift of teaching, which I would never have thought was possible in my early years, as being a teacher puts you front and center in a world where people will want to not only observe you but also evaluate your effectiveness. When I was teaching at a college, I struggled with reading the course feedback because I was afraid of what the students would think about me. Almost 95% of the time, I would get raving reviews about my course content, teaching style, and general helpfulness to my students. But the remaining 5%...ho ho ho! It would take me a few days, maybe even weeks to let go of the sting from someone saying, "She talks too fast" or "She doesn't know what she's talking about."

It would take growth in knowing who I truly was and how the only judgment that mattered really was that from my Father.

Full Glass Practice

- **C.L.E.A.R. Question** - In what ways have you been judged? How have you judged others?
- **Denial** - *The approval of others does not master me; only the approval of Him.*
- **Affirmation** - *I approve of myself and feel great about myself.*
- **Action for the Day**
  o Select an activity that can be accomplished within a relatively short period of time (it may be cleaning up the bedroom, washing the dishes, etc.).
  o As you're doing the activity, take note of how you feel knowing that final approval comes from the Most High.

PART VII

Finances

DAY 21

I Don't Have Enough Money

"Your only Source is the God Presence within you. If your mind is on the Source, the Cause, then the supply flows freely. If your mind is on the effect, you block the flow." - John Randolph Price

While raising my son through grade school, I used to worry myself sick about finances. I was able to manage paying for the core things, but it always seemed I'd fall just a tad short each month. The cost of rent, food, utilities, childcare, doctors' appointments, and school activities was a challenge...and that's with a decent salary and child support. I'm sure any parent can relate.

It sometimes got to a point when I questioned if we would make rent. I worried myself that we would be tossed out on the street and homeless (even though my parents lived a seven-minute drive away and would certainly take us in). I had the limiting belief that there was never enough, and that's what I saw each and every month. In fact, whenever my son would ask for something,

I would reply, "I don't have enough for that." Later, I changed my response to, "It's not in the budget." As he got older, I educated him that "enough" and "budget" are two different things.

Full Glass Practice

- **C.L.E.A.R. Question** – What ways do you feel *you* are not enough? How does that show up in the result of your financial health?
- **Denial** – *Christ Consciousness is not limited.*
- **Affirmation** – *I praise God from whom all blessings flow and flow through me.*
- **Action for the Day**
  - Get still in a quiet place without interruption. Set a time for about 5 minutes.
  - Close your eyes. Envision in your mind's eye all of the love that our dear Father has for you. Sense that He is waiting for you to acknowledge the unlimited resources in time, people, money, and other effects from being in congruence, just waiting for you to pick up The Pitcher.

DAY 22

I'm Not Good at Managing Money

"Wealthy individuals follow the advice of financial experts. It is similar in principle to the idea that if a person's body were sick, he or she would likely seek out a skilled physician for advice." - Bob Proctor

Someone I knew was making the decision to go through a bankruptcy. She shared with me the details of the process; indeed, I even went to one of her appointments with her lawyer. As I sat there listening to the process, I wondered, *was this for me too?* How disappointing it would be as a daughter of whom I considered a financial genius, to have to file for bankruptcy and throw in the towel. Filing for chapter 13 meant that the trajectory of my future would be different from how I planned. It was terrible to claim that I needed that much help, that I needed to give up and couldn't do the financial stuff on my own.

Because of this, I developed the limiting belief that I was terrible at managing money. I knew this was not the case, as I had successfully managed our funds when I was married a decade prior. However, filing for bankruptcy became "real." It felt like evidence of my incapability instead of an option to get back on my feet. I dumped those beliefs and realized that there are factors and circumstances not in our control that may lead to decisions appearing like financial failure. They are not. Each lesson prepares us for greater capacity to hold and manage more in our Glass.

Full Glass Practice

- **C.L.E.A.R. Question** – What education, support, or strategies might you need to be a good servant over your finances?
- **Denial** – *I unfasten the belief of incapability.*
- **Affirmation** – *Divine Life trusts me to be a good steward of all supply.*
- **Action for the Day**
  - Pretend that you earned $1 today, which, in an alternate universe, is a good day's earning.
  - How would you divide up that dollar? How many pennies would go towards food, housing, utilities, giving, fun, entertainment, etc.? Separate those pennies into little stacks on a table.
  - Search online for a good book on money management or re-read one that you may already have.

DAY 23

I Don't Have Enough to Give

"You may be able to give only pennies at first, but give them in the name and the spirit of your opulent God." - Charles Fillmore

One day at church, the talk for that Sunday was about giving. The opening song for the day had lyrics speaking about worries of lack, and the action to take is to give that very thing away. Whatever that may be. Love, encouragement, even money. It is a test of faith to let go of the worry that there isn't enough money to pay the bills, yet be assured that we will always provide our share to our church, loved ones, and charities that are important to us.

I was aware of the premise and even read several books about it. However, there was a part of me that lacked the faith to see how this would work. *Ye of little faith.* Once I did start to release the worry and took sheer joy out of giving, something remarkable started to happen. I seemed to have enough money to give while also taking care of the usual household expenses and finance fun experiences. Nothing else changed in income.

Full Glass Practice

- **C.L.E.A.R. Question** - What holds you back from giving of your time, finances, or other gifts of your wealth?
- **Denial** - *I deny that any form of giving is not useful.*
- **Affirmation** - *I live in unlimited abundance and share my gifts with joy.*
- **Action for the Day**
  o Remember that $1 from yesterday? Great! Pay yourself again today and give each penny of that dollar a job like before.
  o Take the designated amount you put aside for giving and ensure that you do so. Whether at church, to a person, or in one of those donation boxes found at grocery and convenience stores.

DAY 24

Rich People Are [Insert Negative Thought Here]

"Money will only make you more of what you already are." - T. Harv Eker

I just don't get it. I hear people complain about how the rich get richer and the poor get poorer. How the rich are thieves and crooks that only look out for themselves. The lists of negative expressions and thoughts about the rich and being rich are exhausting. Yet I'll also hear the same folks talk about how they can't wait to win the lottery or play a casino game in the hopes of winning their luck. Or perhaps they work hard, dedicating themselves to something creative and meaningful so that they can move up the ladder and earn more money. However, what sense is there to be something that you despise?

We need to work on removing the limiting belief that being rich is a bad thing, as there is so much good that can come from it, as long as we remember the true source of our wealth. It's not the job. It's not the business. It's not the investment. It's the guidance and grace of the Almighty Provider. When we focus our minds on that, we realize He'll supply for our needs as well as the ability to take care of others.

Full Glass Practice

- **C.L.E.A.R. Question** - What are your opinions about rich people? Do you want to be rich? Is being rich more than just monetary wealth for you?
- **Denial** - *Wealth does not rule me and is only an effect.*
- **Affirmation** - *Blessings of wealth come to me so that I may better serve.*
- **Action for the Day**
  o Go online and do some research about individuals and couples who demonstrate philanthropic ways of using their abundance (there are more than you think).
  o Did you see consistencies throughout their giving (not just a one-time thing)?

PART VIII

Creative Expression & Success

DAY 25

I Don't Have Enough Experience

"Self-doubt undermines the process of finding your gifts and sharing them with the world. Moreover, if developing and sharing our gifts is how we honor spirit and connect with God, self-doubt is letting our fear undermine our faith." - Brené Brown

One day at church, I was looking at the bulletin when the Reverend referred us to the highlighted ministry of the month, the media ministry, as it explained about the sound, lighting, and even social media needs that the ministry is responsible for. Hmmmm...social media? That's my jam! Sounds and lighting! I used to be on stage crew in school and loved my small acts as a performer on a stage. I was very interested. However, I talked myself out of it, as I had plenty of responsibility and committed projects on my plate and didn't want to over-commit. For some strange reason, I still doubted my experience.

The thought lingered for a bit during my drive home. A week later, lying in bed that early Sunday morning, the thought came back. *You should join the media ministry.* I told myself no, I've got plenty of other things to do; let me just enjoy church services and find other ways to engage and serve on a lighter basis. Still lying in bed, the thought came back. *You NEED to join the media ministry.* Well, I was not so sure about that, and just as that last thought came to my head, I felt another prompt, almost like a nagging parent who wants you to get you out of bed. *You...* *"Okay, already!"* I said to the Holy Spirit, wrestling with my bedcovers, hopping out of bed in faith and got myself ready for church. I made my commitment and enjoyed every little bit of actively serving the church from behind the scenes. Pure joy.

Fast forward to the final editing of this book, and we are in the midst of the Covid-19 pandemic. Like the rest of the world, our church has had to come to terms with a new norm. The most revealing string of events came when our church leaders realized that things were brewing and that we needed to make some plans to use technology before all hell literally started to break loose. It appeared that my experience with online video and social media platforms would be very useful.

A month later, I didn't even realize how much that service was needed. I had so much doubt and resisted listening to the Still Small Voice (that was getting louder by the moment). Had I continued to doubt my capacity and experience to serve, I would not have been present and prepared to assist our church in the continued blessing of the Spirit. So amazing how He works!

Full Glass Practice

- **C.L.E.A.R. Question** – What opportunities have come up in your life where you doubt that you have the experience?
- **Denial** – *There are some things that I know and know how to do. Others, not so much.*

- **Affirmation** - *I start where I am. I use what I have. I do what I can.*
- **Action for the Day**
  - o Take some significant time to write down a few opportunities that you may be able to reexamine.
  - o Get still and pray and meditate on these opportunities.
  - o Take note if the Holy Spirit is speaking to you.

DAY 26

I'll Never Achieve Success

"Your Soul is the destination - and your feelings are the road signs directing you to it. Your feelings lead you home by giving you moment-by-moment signals." - Danielle Laporte

If we want to work on what we should be doing, we need to first figure out why the heck we want to be doing it in the first place. I was once coaching a client who was struggling with that very thing, even though he did not realize it. He wanted me to help him prepare for an important job interview. We went through the usual preparations about assessing his skills, talents, interests, and hobbies. Which all can be related to who he was, as a person and professional. However, when it came to talking about his career goals, he gave me a canned generic answer that was boring. He wanted to utilize his skills in serving guests and taking care of employees in a healthy way. Boring! I had to help him dig deep to understand what he REALLY wanted. Did he want to feel helpful? Fulfilled? What was his angle? Why did he really want these things? I kept asking why, why, why, until we got to the core of what he really wanted in life.

For those of us who are emotionally sensitive, we may do things out of obligation for others. We don't want to be hurt. We don't want to make ourselves too vulnerable. Doing makes us vulnerable because it opens the door to failure. WE don't want that! That's a death sentence! What if we do the wrong thing? How would we survive such a fuddle? What if the doing is not in line with our core values? What if what we're doing is against our family's wishes (because again, we don't want to disappoint our family and friends)? It took me some time to be able to realize what others wanted me to do, implied or not, and just do my own darn thing. I had to let go of the fear that I would disappoint, let down, or get rejected by the most important people in my life. I also didn't want that to happen with the surface-level relationships that I had because that was even worse!

Full Glass Practice

- **C.L.E.A.R. Question** – Do you have clear goals for what you want to achieve and manifest in your life?
- **Denial** – *I pull out the weeds in my mind of lack of success.*
- **Affirmation** – *I take pride in what I've accomplished and look forward to the next step.*
- **Action for the Day**
  - o Carve out about an hour to list some of your past achievements.
  - o Can you recall if these achievements were done on your own desire or someone else's?
  - o What would be the next step in a goal you want to achieve now—for you?

DAY 27

Not Trying is Better Than Failing

"Don't worry about failures; worry about the chances you miss when you don't even try." - Jack Canfield

F ind at least one moment to be present and be in joy! Seize that moment. Revel in God's blessings. Occasionally, I get still and relish in the goodness that is happening in my life. How truly sweet it is to be loved by Divine Life and realize that all things are in divine order. Of course, this is usually from an enlightened perspective. However, occasionally, it is in the present moment. Which is why mindfulness, and I don't only mean meditation, is so valuable. Mindfulness is about being present and paying attention to what is the here and now. In staying present, you notice the light coming in through the window, the sound of the heater in your home, the feel of your breath coming out of your nose. It's realizing that life is happening in the here and now, and you have an opportunity to experience. Not to think about the past, not to think about the future, but to only think about what is happening right now. From there, you are seizing the day, *carpe diem*, seizing the beautiful little moments that are happening to you. It is truly a beautiful thing.

In these moments, I am not afraid. God is here. Jesus' teachings make sense. Everything makes sense, and I am no longer afraid. I am the blessed daughter of the Most High. I can be nothing, and I can be everything. I can do nothing, and I can do it all. I can have nothing, and I can have it all. It's as if time and space no longer matter. It is a human construct that has no meaning in the heavenly, universal realm.

Even as I write these words, my eyes are welled up, and I feel a sense of peace and awe. God is working in and through me to express, and I know that it is all in divine order. So, why in the world did I find ways to put a dump heap on my bliss? Why had I feared doing, being, and having when it is all there? Why have I feared NOT doing, being, and having? Can I be content with being content?

Full Glass Practice

- **C.L.E.A.R. Question** – Is there an achievement you wished you could have met, but did not? What were the factors that led to the lack of success?
- **Denial** – *Failing is not proof of future worthiness to success.*
- **Affirmation** – *I know what my values are, and I'm confident of the decisions I make.*
- **Action for the Day**
  - Make a decision to try something new. This may have to be scheduled over the course of a week.
  - For today, take one very simple action (or two) that would move you closer to that goal.

DAY 28

What if I'm Successful?

"God did not give us a spirit that makes us afraid
but a spirit of power and love and self-control."
-2 Timothy 1:7 NCV

My ultimate fear is not of failing, but of succeeding! The
rolling questions that had been on my mind were:

- What if I achieved my biggest life goals?
- How would that change me?
- Would people change how they related to me?
- Would it change how I related to them?
- Or maybe someone would find out...dunh...dunh...
  dunh! That I'm an imposter.

The imposter syndrome was running deep within me for a
long time. It's part of why it's taken me three years to settle down
and complete this book. Divine Inspiration led me down this
path. However, it was my own will that kept holding me back.
I kept telling myself I wasn't ready. What did I know? Would

people even care what I have to say? Who am I to talk about emotional wellness, stress, and spiritual revelations? Duh.

So, I realized that God speaks through all of us and that if I continue to align myself with Him, I am not an imposter.

Full Glass Practice

- **C.L.E.A.R. Question –** What do you think will happen when you achieve success in your next goal? What might be the result?
- **Denial –** *I eliminate the fear that I don't deserve success.*
- **Affirmation –** *Achievement and success draw me closer to the next phase of God's plans in my journey.*
- **Action for the Day**
  o Jot down in a journal or notebook gratitude for the success you've achieved in a particular goal that you are working towards.
  o Express gratitude to God for allowing you to be a vehicle for His work.

FINAL THOUGHTS - DAY 29 AND BEYOND

Celebrate! You've completed the end of this program and should be very proud of yourself. If you found that you jumped and skipped around the book, no worries; be proud of that too. As we conclude this part of our journey, I leave you with this final advice:

Lather. Rinse and Repeat, as desired.

Dumping our limiting beliefs is a life-long journey. We move forward, we slip. We clean and polish Our Glass, refresh with New Water and receive from The Pitcher. We learn new ways of thinking and believing, sometimes we need to be reminded. The limiting beliefs presented here are just a sampling. This is why I provided a free online course so that you can review the concepts and dive deeper in exploration of the beliefs that hold you back. The *Full Glass Living Companion Course* at *fullglassliving.com* was curated as a helpful way to do just that. With the newfound concept of Full Glass Living and the insights provided, I wish you many blessings on your journey to an enlightened understanding of your Good. And so it is. Amen.

REFERENCES AND SUGGESTED READING

(1991). *The Holy Bible, New Century Version.* Dallas, Texas: Word Publishing.

(1982). *The Holy Bible, New King James Version.* Thomas Nelson, Inc.

Abrahamsson, I. (2012). *Sensitivity unveiled: Your unrecognized power.* Morrisville, NC: Lulu Publishing.

Barrett, L. (2017). *How emotions are made: The secret life of the brain.* New York, NY: Houghton Mifflin Harcourt.

Brown, B. (2010). *The Gifts of Imperfection: Let go of who you think you're supposed to be and embrace who you are.* Center City, MI: Hazelden.

Cady, E. H. (1896). *Lessons in truth: A course of twelve lessons in practical Christianity.* Kansas City, MO: Unity Movement.

Carter, C. (2017). *The Sweet Spot: How to accomplish more by doing less.* New York, NY: Ballantine Books.

Colbert, D. (2003). *Deadly motions: Understand the mind-body-spirit connection that can heal or destroy you.* Nashville, TN: Thomas Nelson Publishers.

Dweck, C. (2006). *Mindset: The new psychology of success.* New York, NY: Ballatine Books.

Di Santo, H. (2015). *I should be happy but I'm not: The 6 practices of emotionally fit people.* Surrey Hill, VIC, Australia: Michael Hanrahan Publishing.

Enlighten (Eds). (2017). *Emotions & essential oils: A reference guide for emotional healing (6ᵗʰ ed).* Salt Lake City, UT: Enlighten Alternative Healing, LLC.

Fillmore, C. (2007). *Prosperity.* Unity Village, Missouri: Unity House.

Green, J., & Longman III, T. (1996). *The Everyday Study Bible: For people who want to know the word.* Dallas, Texas: World Publishing, Inc.

Goleman, D. (1995). *Emotional intelligence: Why it can matter more than IQ.* New York, NY: Bantam Books.

Hall, K. (2004). *The emotionally sensitive person; Finding peace when your emotions overwhelm you.* Oakland, CA: New Harbinger Publications, Inc.

Hausmann, W.W. (2010). *Discover your God-given potential: 12 spiritual abilities to change your life.* Unity Village, MO: Unity.

Hay, L. (1988). *Heal your body: The mental causes for physical illness and the metaphysical way to overcome them.* Carlsbad, CA: Hay House, Inc.

Lindner, K. (2013). *Your killer emotions: The 7 steps to mastering the toxic emotions, urges, and impulses that sabotage you.* Austin, Texas: GreenLeaf Book Press.

Maxwell, J.C. (2007). *The 21 irrefutable laws of leadership: Follow them and people will follow you Nashville,* TN: Thomas Nelson.

Maxwell, J.C. (2007). *The Maxwell Leadership Bible: Lessons in leadership from the word of God.* Duluth, Georgia: Maxwell Motivation, Inc.

Moorjani, A. (2016). *What if this is Heaven?: How our cultural myths prevent us from experiencing heaven on earth.* Carlsbad, CA: Hay House, Inc.

Orloof, J. (2017). The empath's survival guide: Life strategies for sensitive people. Boulder, CO: Sounds True.

Ortner, N. (2013). *The tapping solution: A revolutionary system for stress-free living.* Carlsbad, CA: Hay House, Inc.

Proctor, B. (2002). *You were born rich.* Scottsdale, AZ: LifeSuccess Productions.

Price, J. (1987). *The abundance book.* Carlsbad, CA: Hay House, Inc.

Sawyer, H. (2015). *Highly Intuitive People: 7 right-brain traits to change the lives of intuitive-sensitive people.* Carlsbad, CA: Hay House, Inc.

Schneider, B. (2008). *Energy Leadership: Transforming your workplace and your life from the core.* Hoboken NJ: John Wiley & Sons, Inc.

Solie, L. (2013). *Take charge of your emotions: Seven steps to overcoming depression, anxiety, and anger.* Minneapolis, MN: Bethany House.

Warren, R. (2002). *The purpose driven life: What on earth am I here for?* Grand Rapids, MI: Zaondervan.

Wheatley, M. (2006). *Leadership and the new science: Discovering order in a chaotic world (3rd ed).* San Francisco, CA: Berrett-Koehler Publishers, Inc.

Wordwood, V. (1996). *The fragrant mind: Aromatherapy for personality, mind, mood, and emotion.* Novato, CA: New World Library.

Wordwood, V. (1999). *Aromatherapy for the soul: Healing the spirit with fragrance and essential oils.* Novato, CA: New World Library.

Printed in the United States
By Bookmasters